Real World
Colouring Book
For Advanced Users & Adults

50 Images

**Created From Real Life Photos
For You To Colour As You Please.**

ISBN 978-0-359-97215-9
90000
9 780359 972159

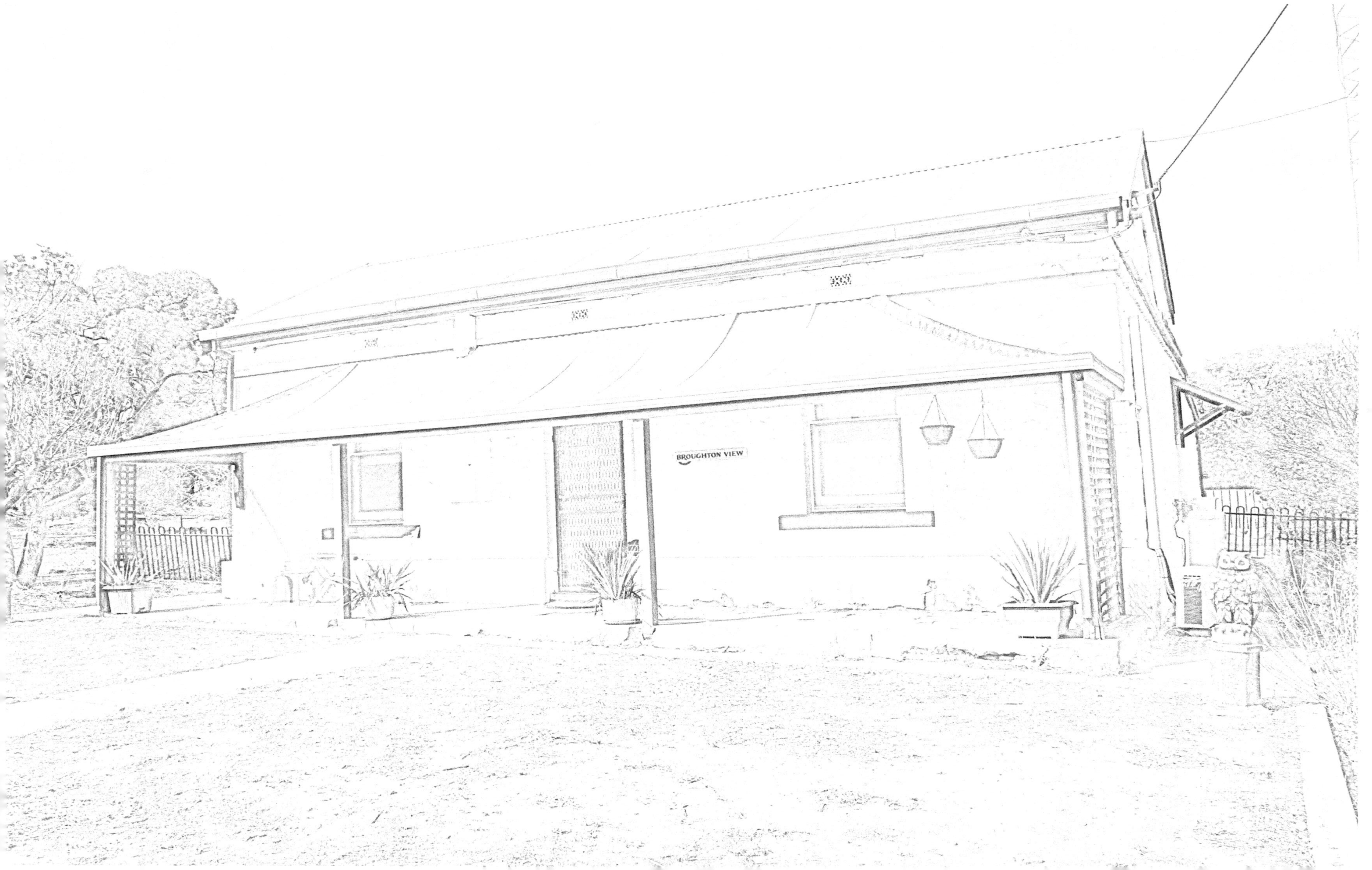
BROUGHTON VIEW

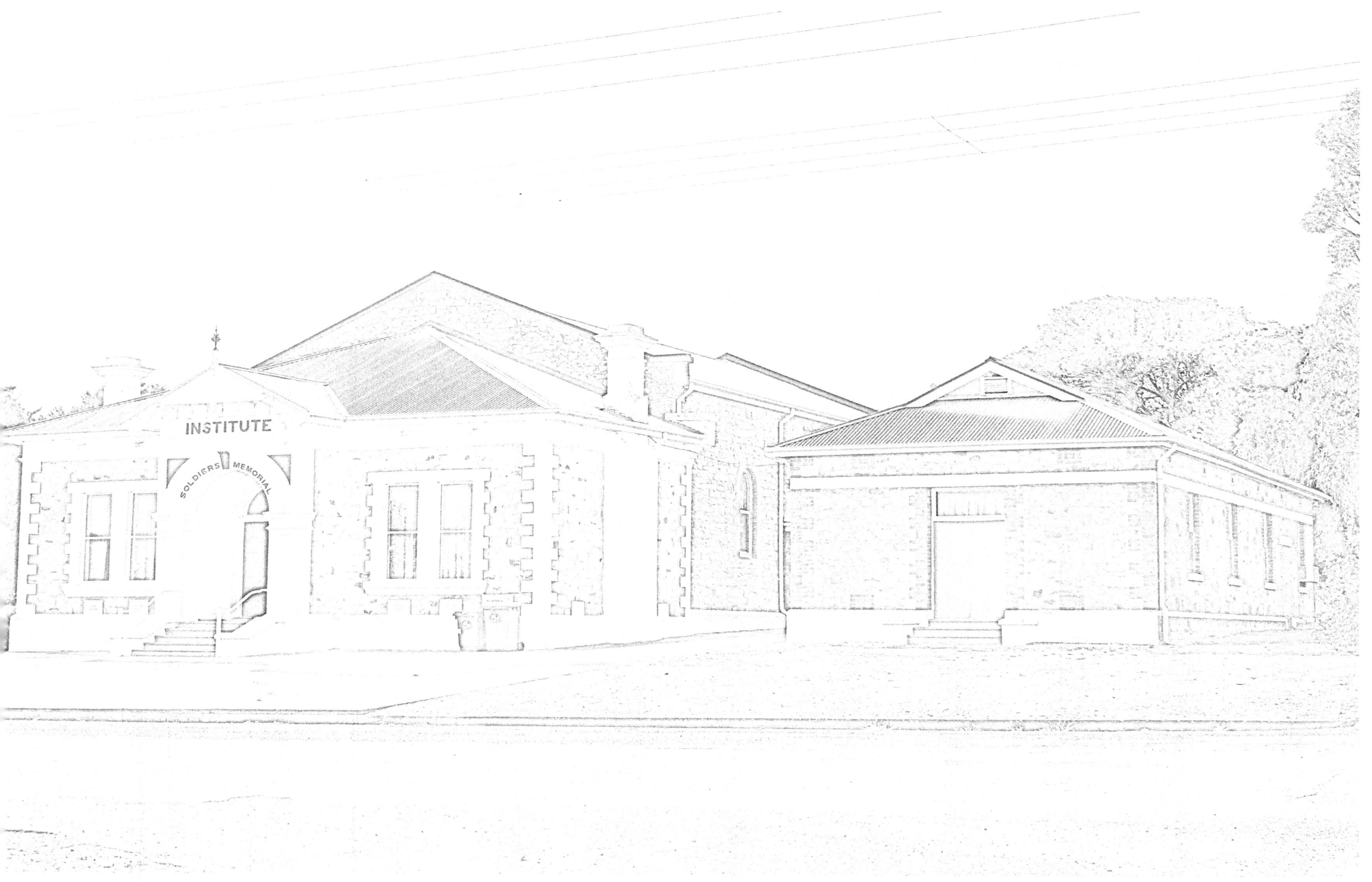
INSTITUTE
SOLDIERS MEMORIAL

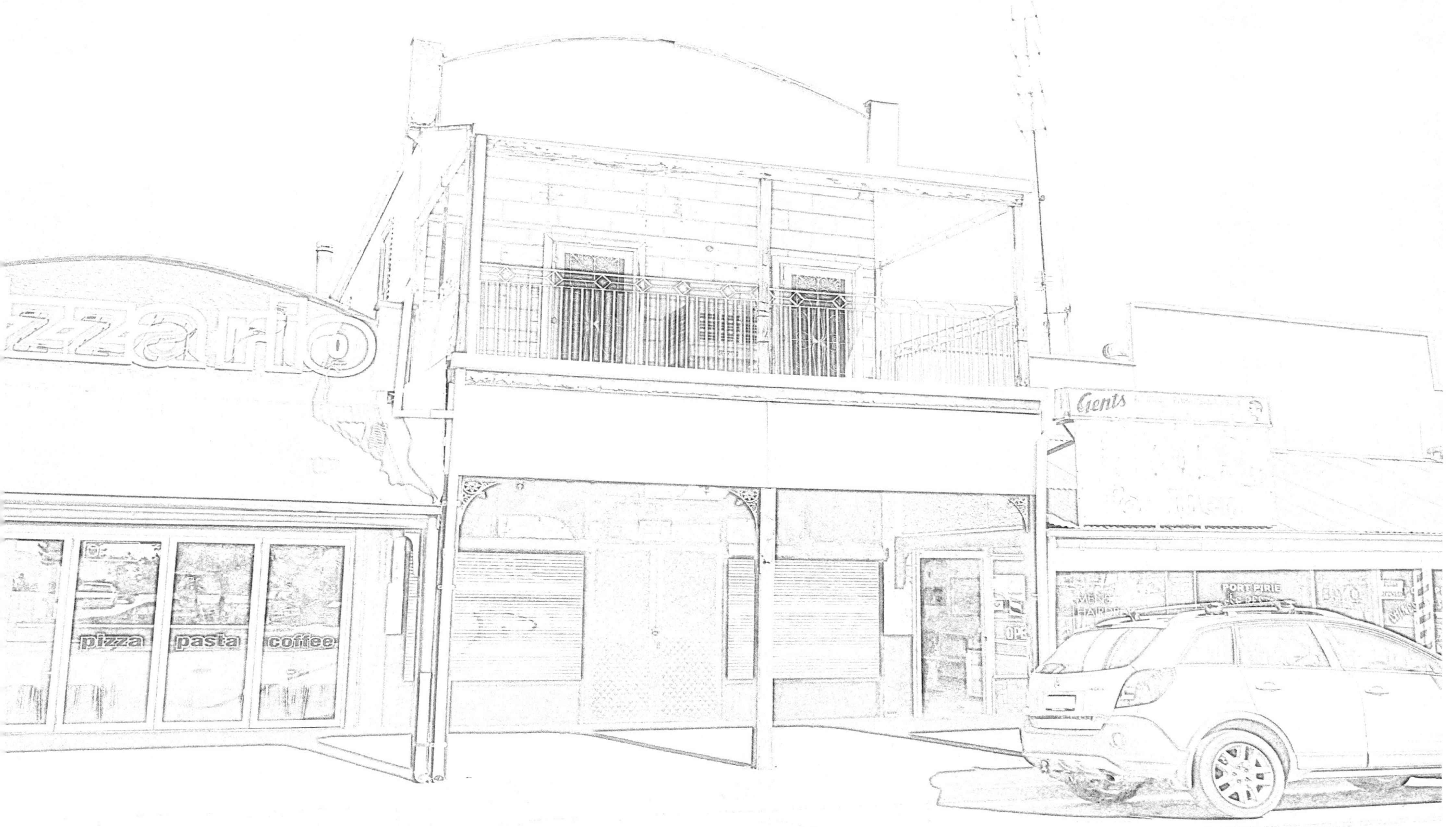

zzario
pizza
pasta
coffee
Gents
PORT PIRIE

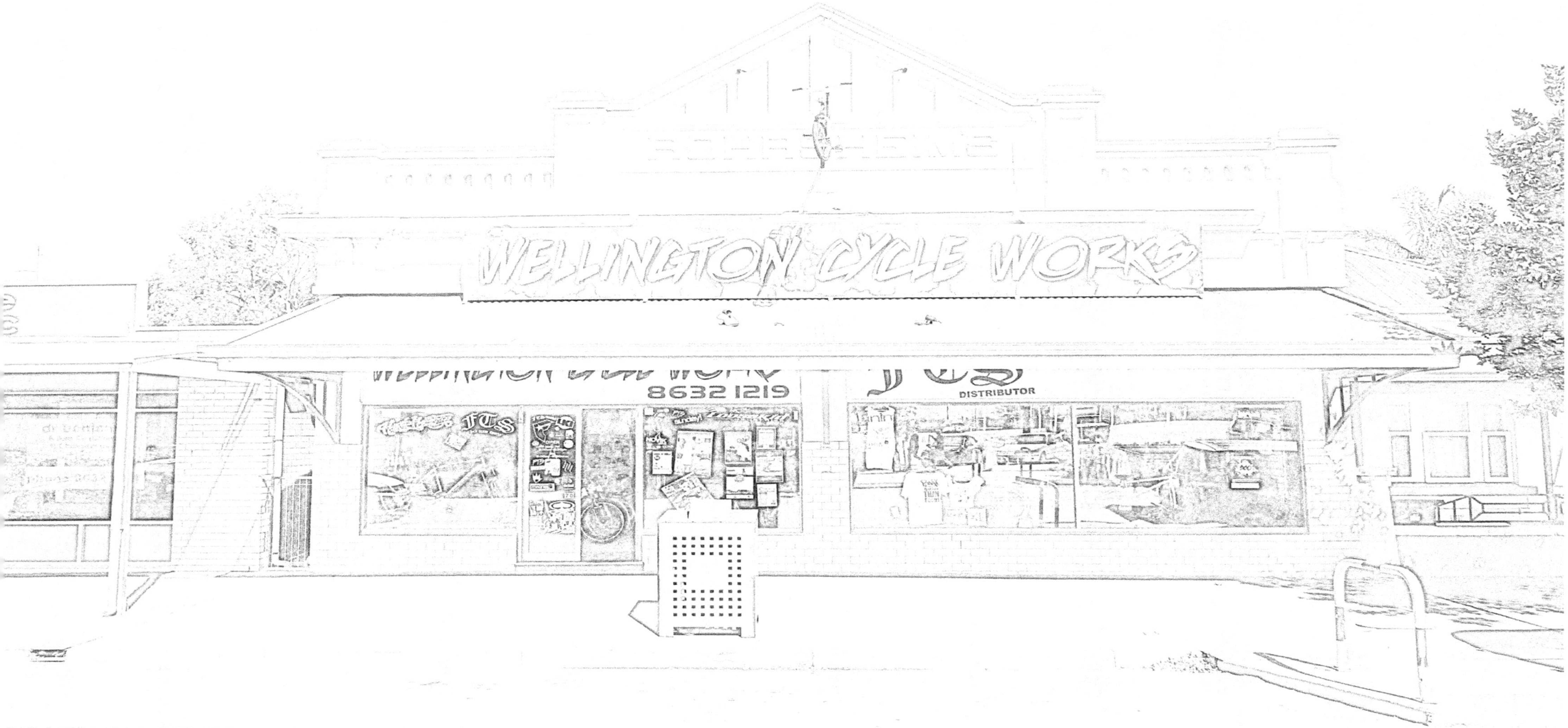
WELLINGTON CYCLE WORKS
8632 1219
DISTRIBUTOR

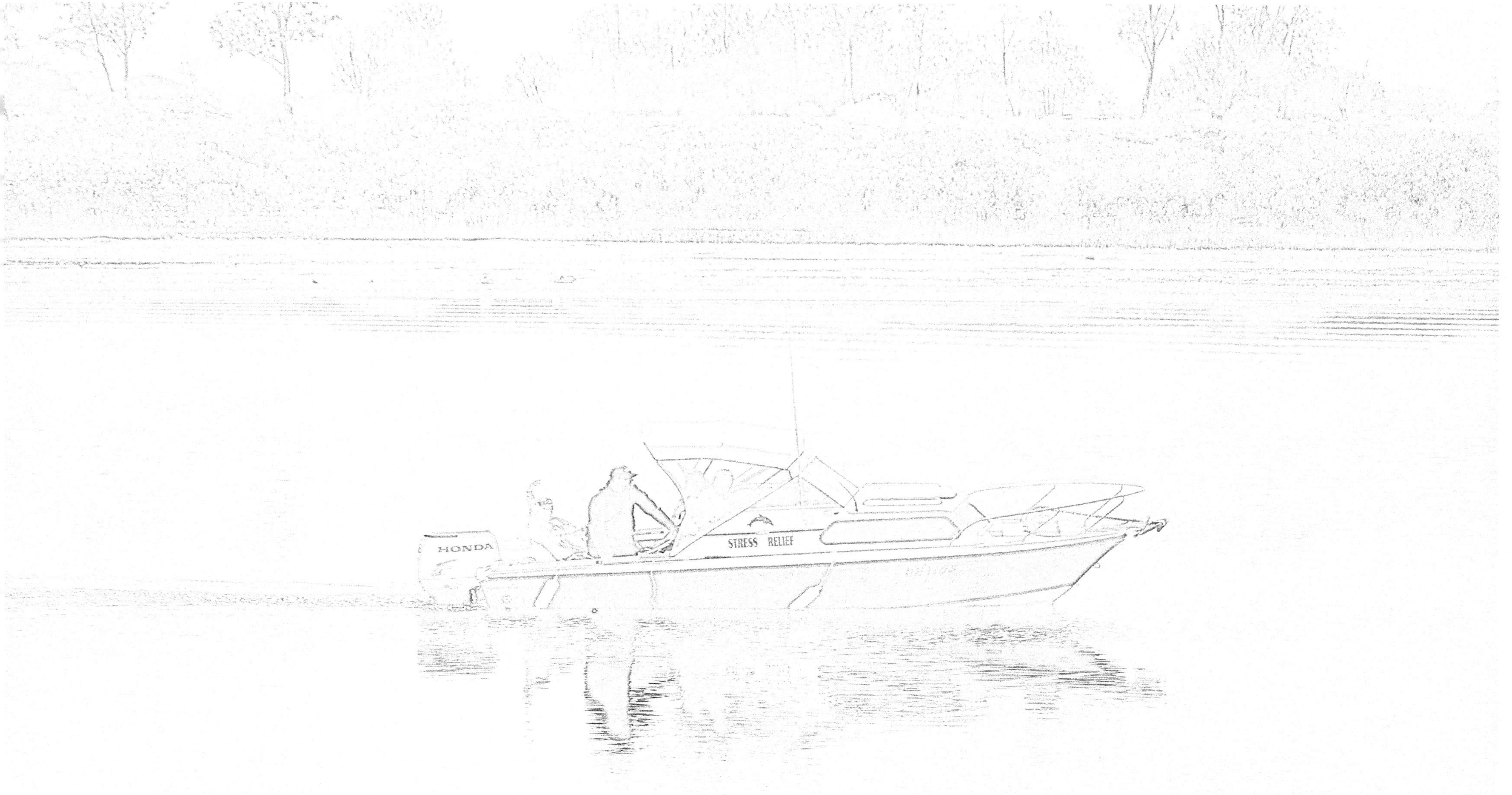
HONDA
STRESS RELIEF

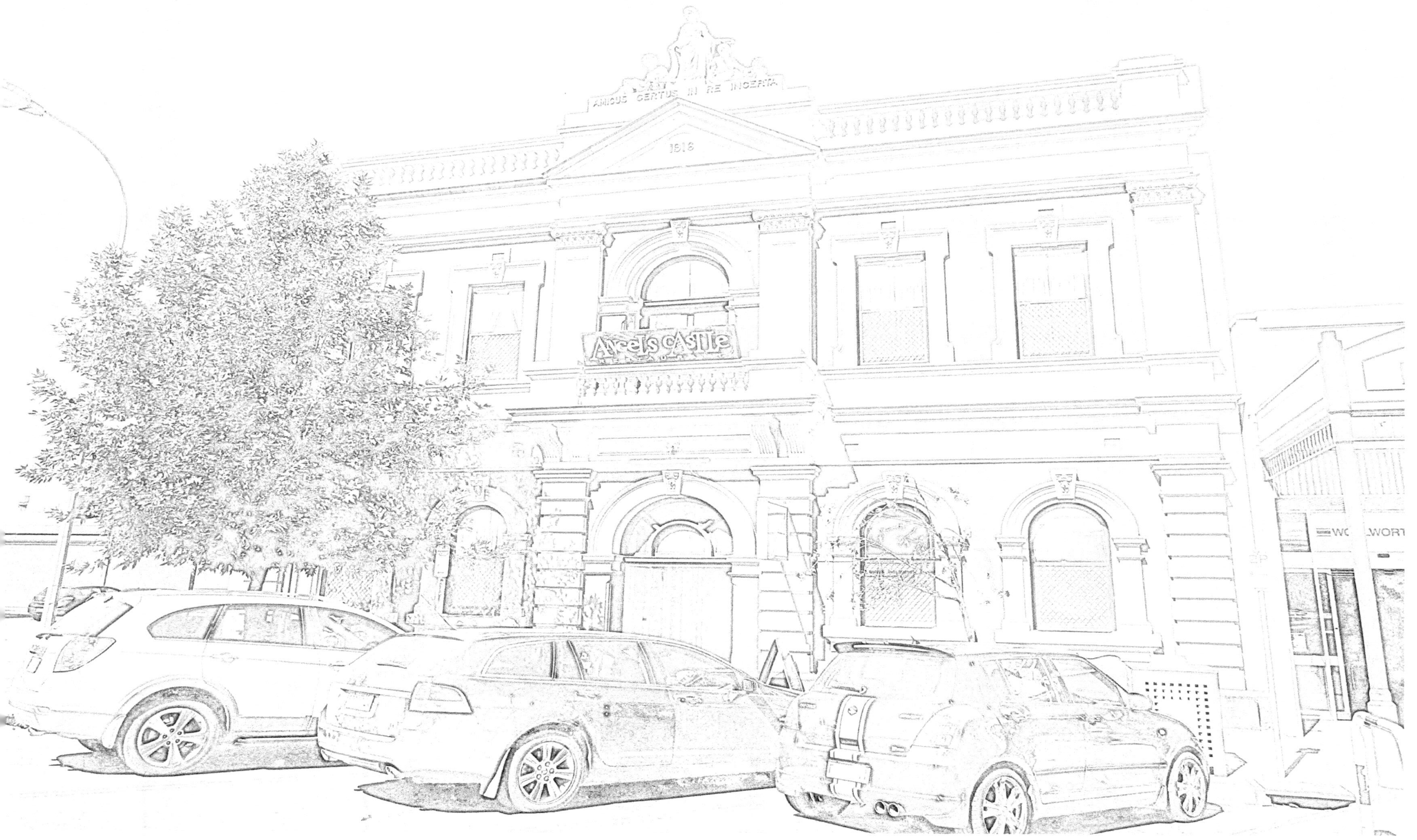
AMICUS CERTUS IN RE INCERTA
1918
Ayer's cASTle

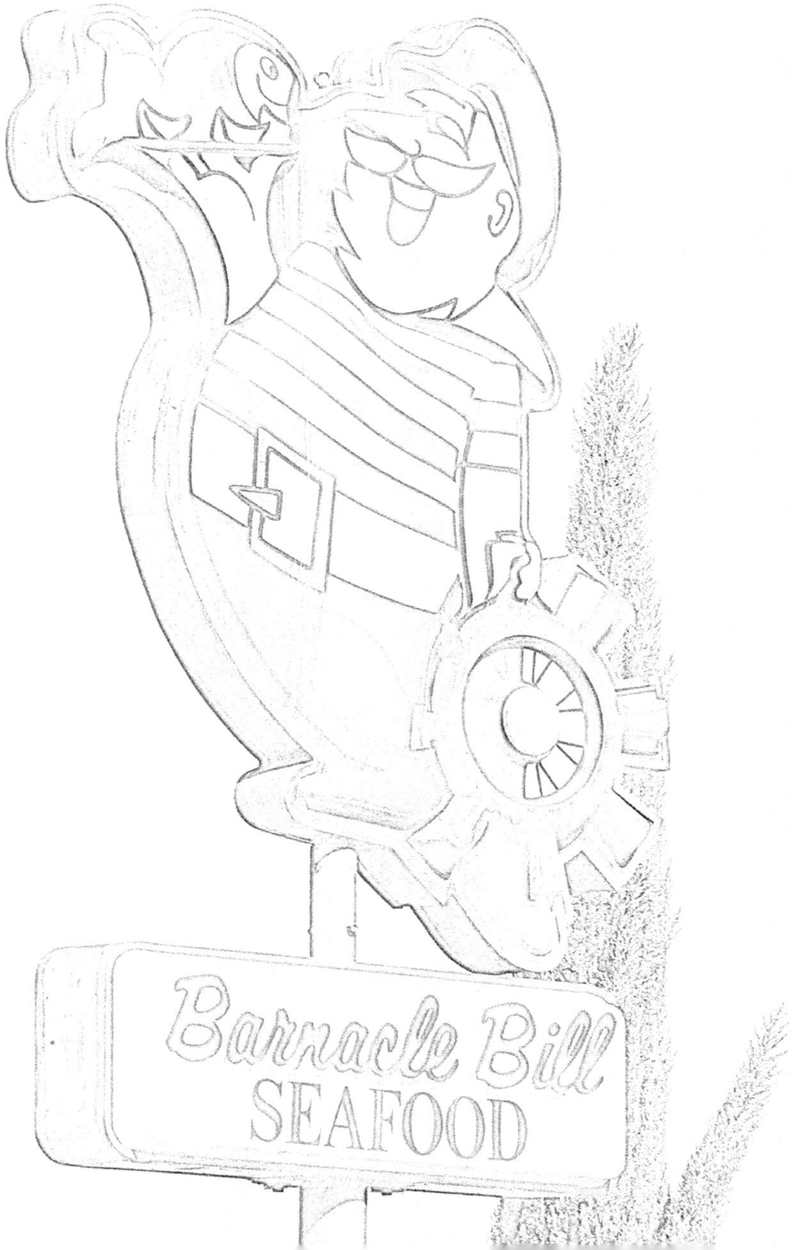
Barnacle Bill
SEAFOOD

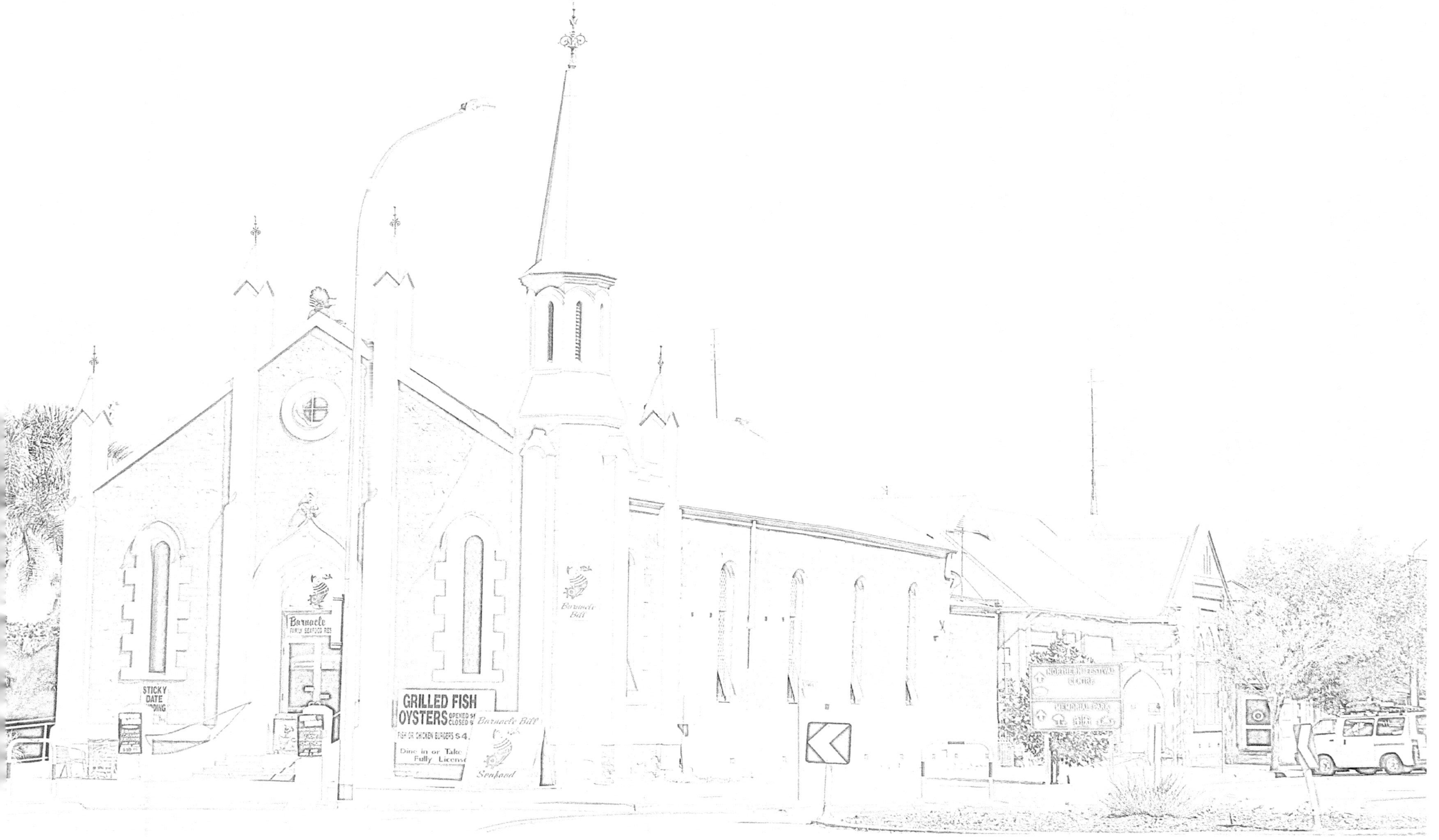
STICKY
DATE
Barnacle
GRILLED FISH
OYSTERS
Barnacle Bill
Dine in or Take
Seafood
Barnacle
Bill
NORTHERN FESTIVAL
CENTRE
MEMORIAL PARK

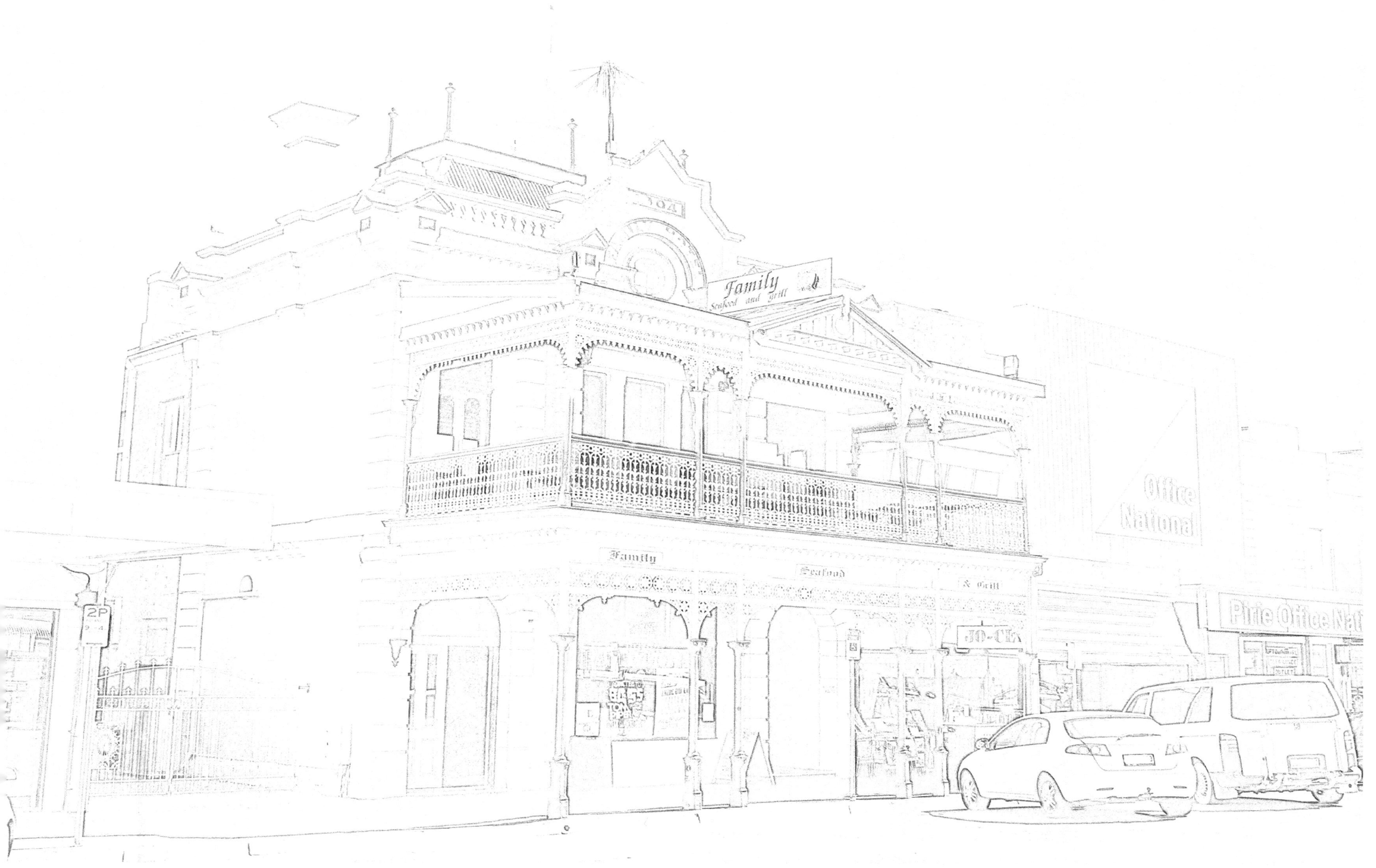
Family
Seafood and Grill
Family
Seafood
& Grill
Office National
Pirie Office Nat
2P

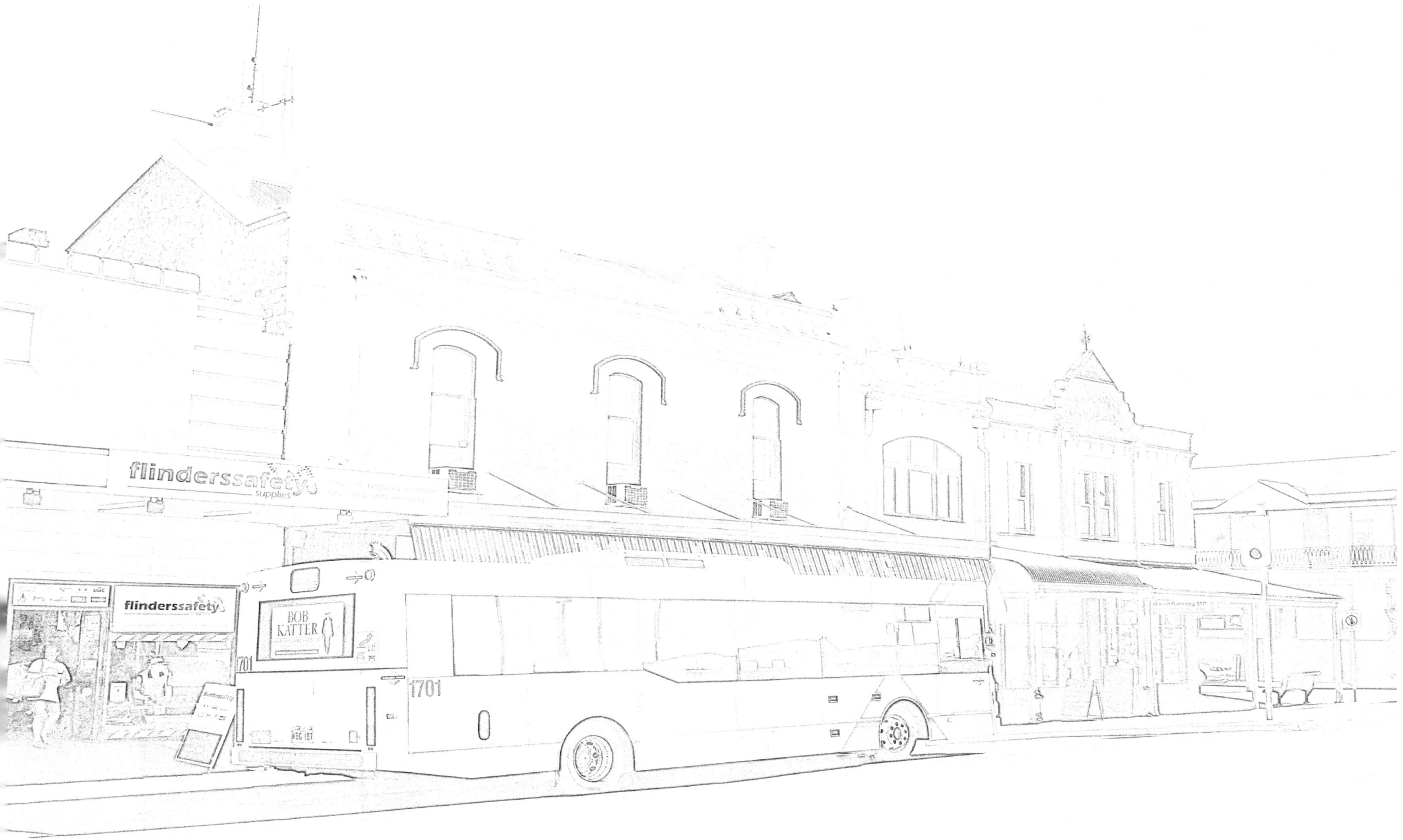
flinderssafety
supplies
flinderssafety
BOB
KATTER
1701
1701

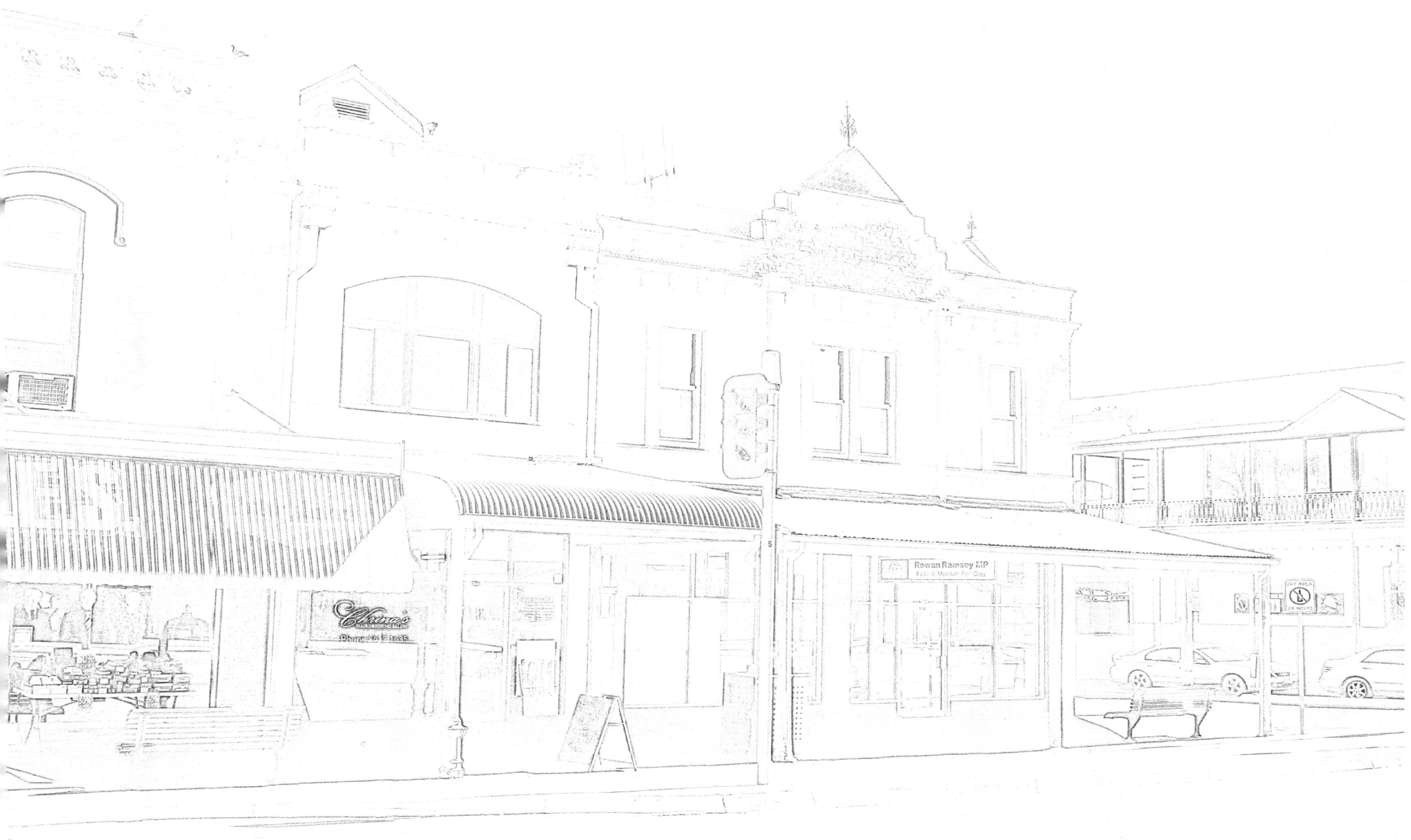
Rowan Ramsey MP
Federal Member For Grey

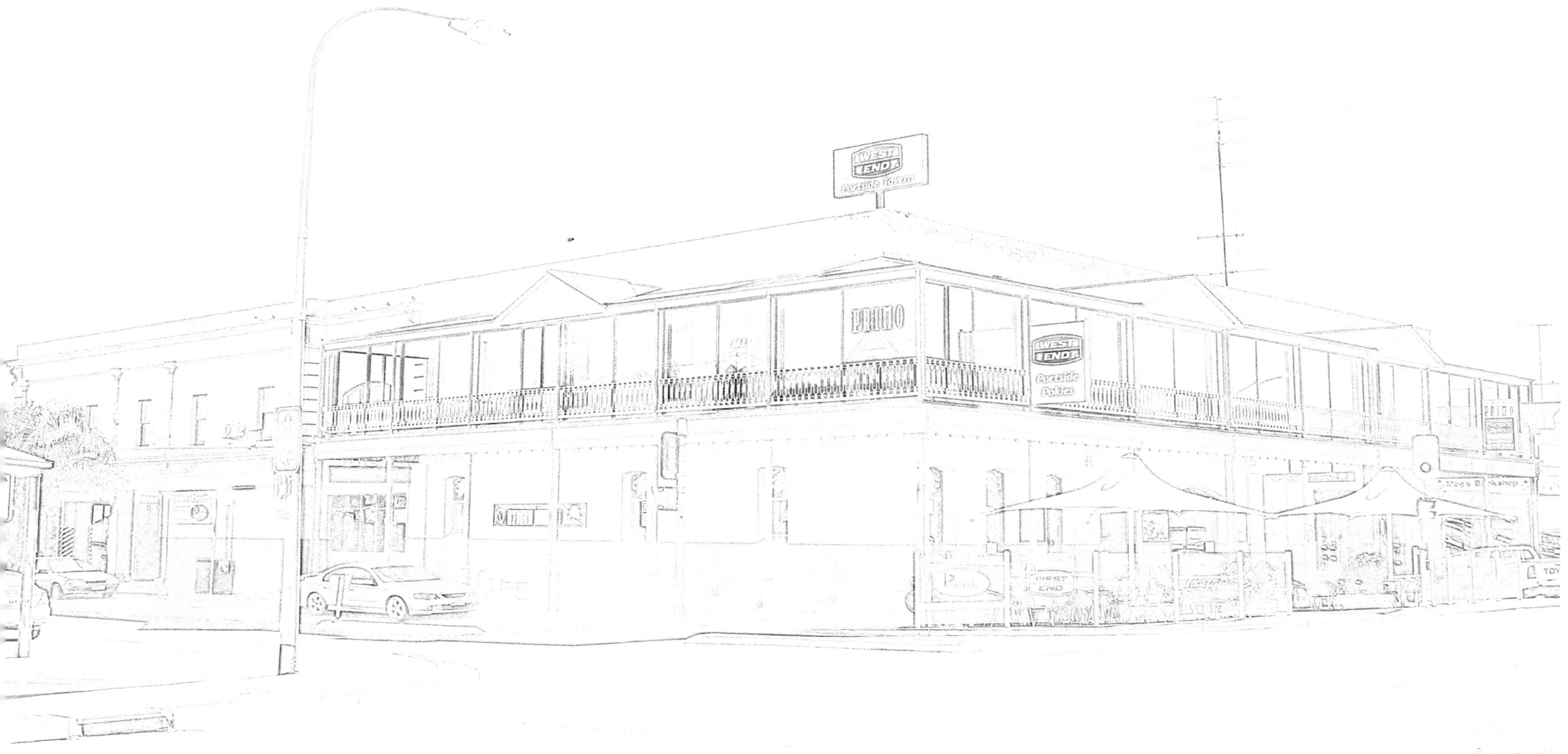
WEST END
Portside Tavern
PROMO
WEST END
Portside Pokies
Meg's Bookshop

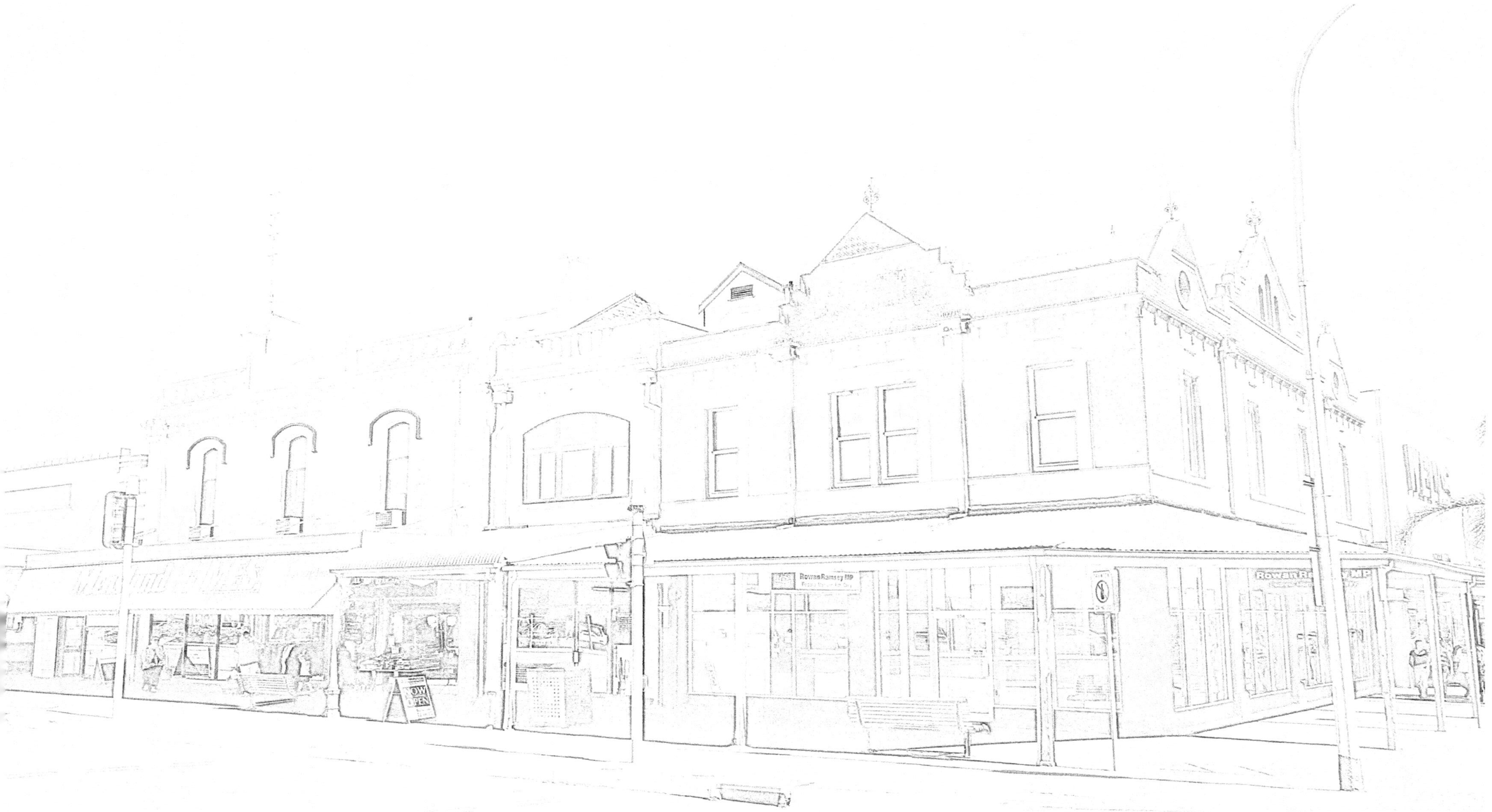
Rowan Ramsey MP
NOW OPEN

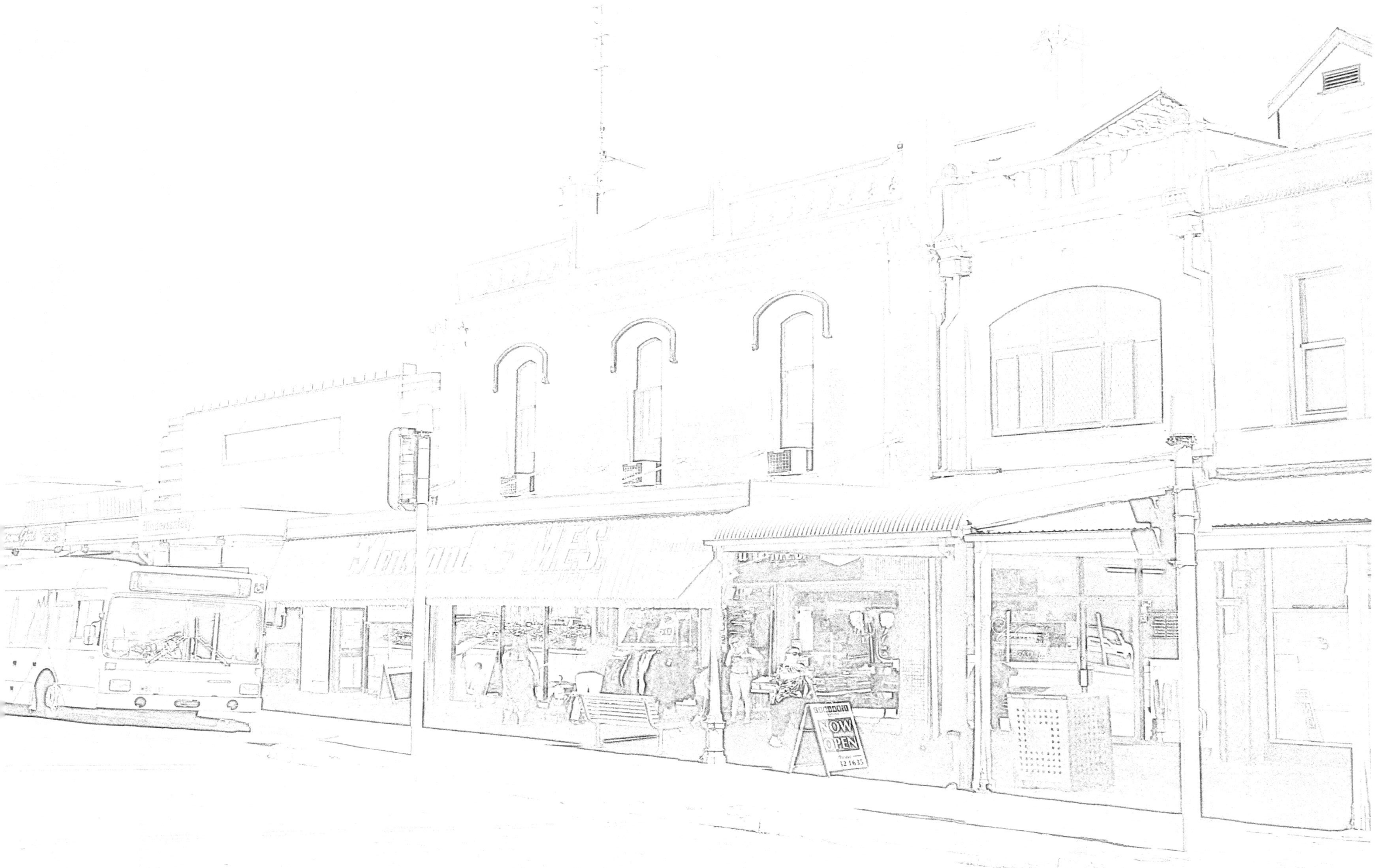
NOW
OPEN

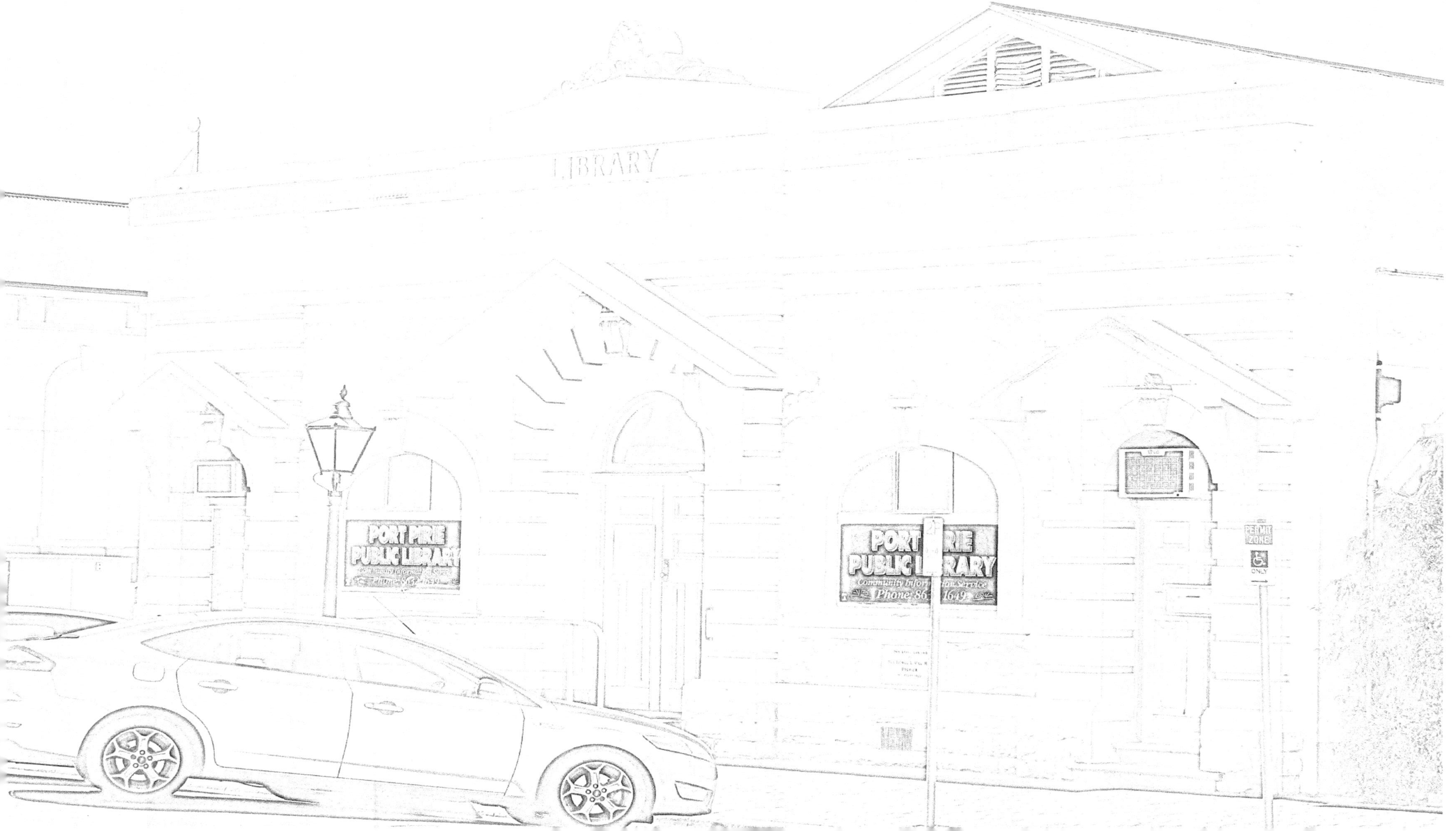
LIBRARY
PORT PIRIE
PUBLIC LIBRARY
PORT PIRIE
PUBLIC LIBRARY
Community Information Service
PERMIT ZONE
ONLY

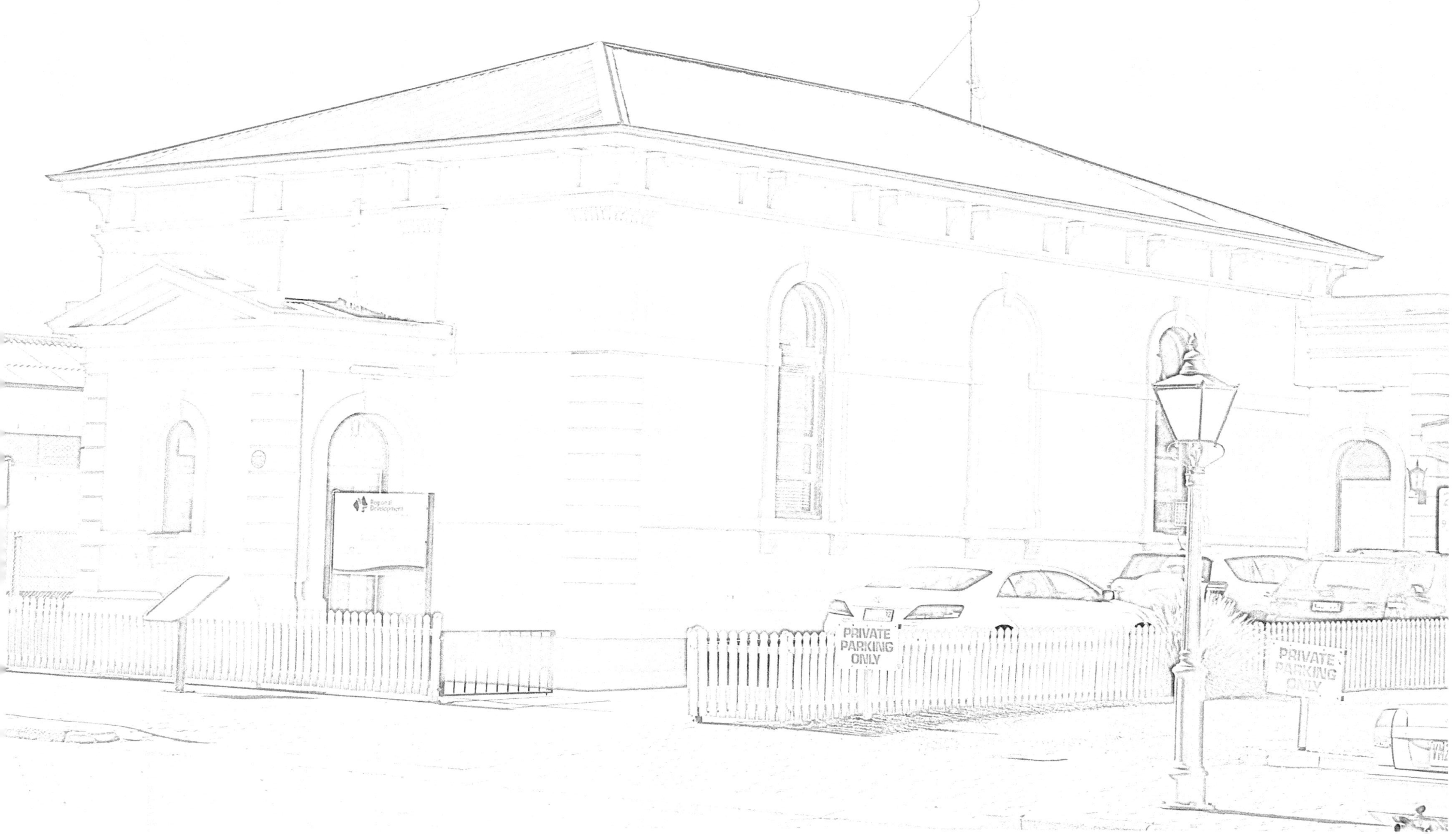
Regional Development
PRIVATE PARKING ONLY
PRIVATE PARKING ONLY

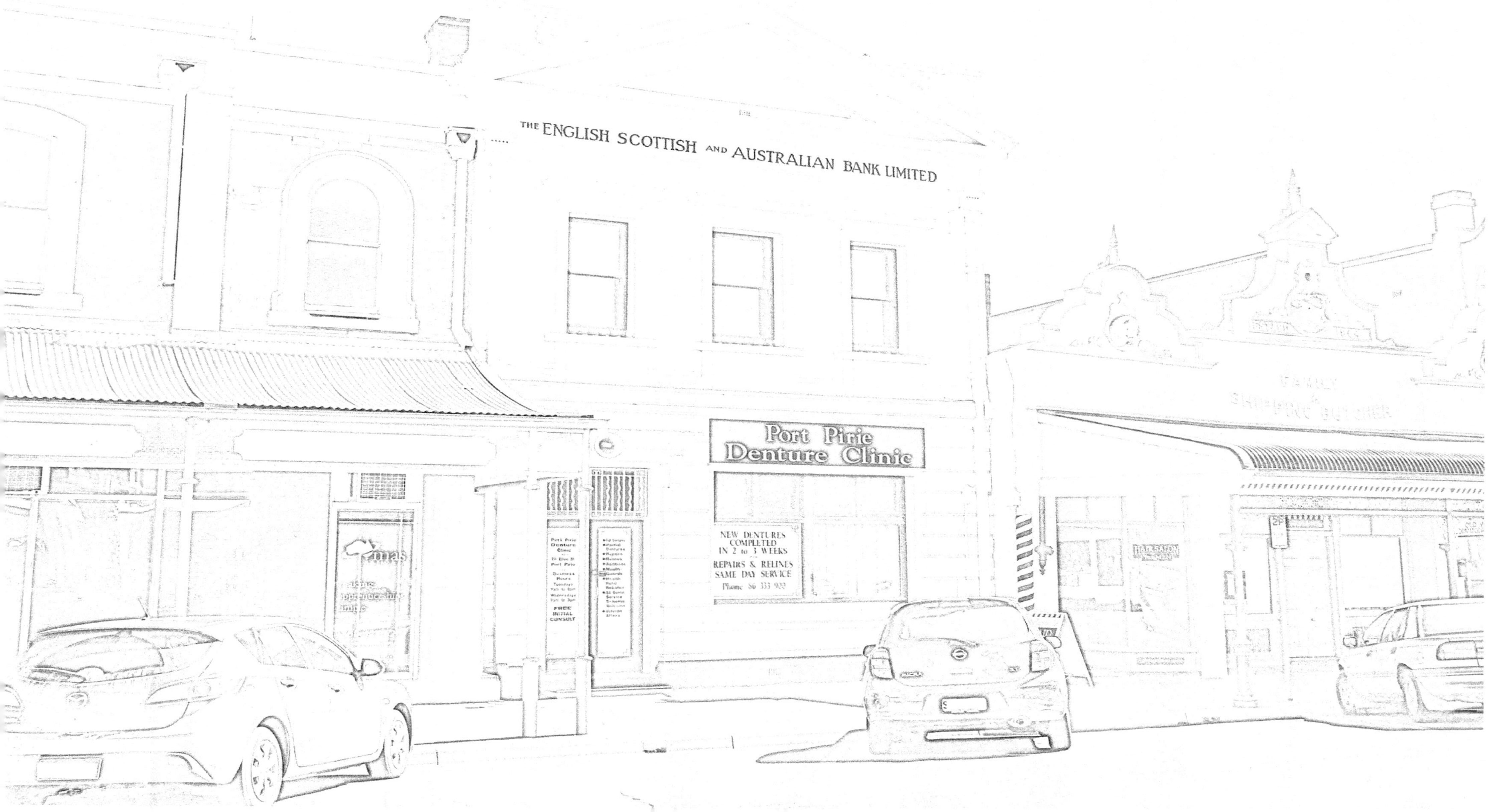
THE ENGLISH SCOTTISH AND AUSTRALIAN BANK LIMITED
Port Pirie Denture Clinic
NEW DENTURES COMPLETED IN 2 to 3 WEEKS
REPAIRS & RELINES SAME DAY SERVICE
Phone 86 333 922
FREE INITIAL CONSULT
2P

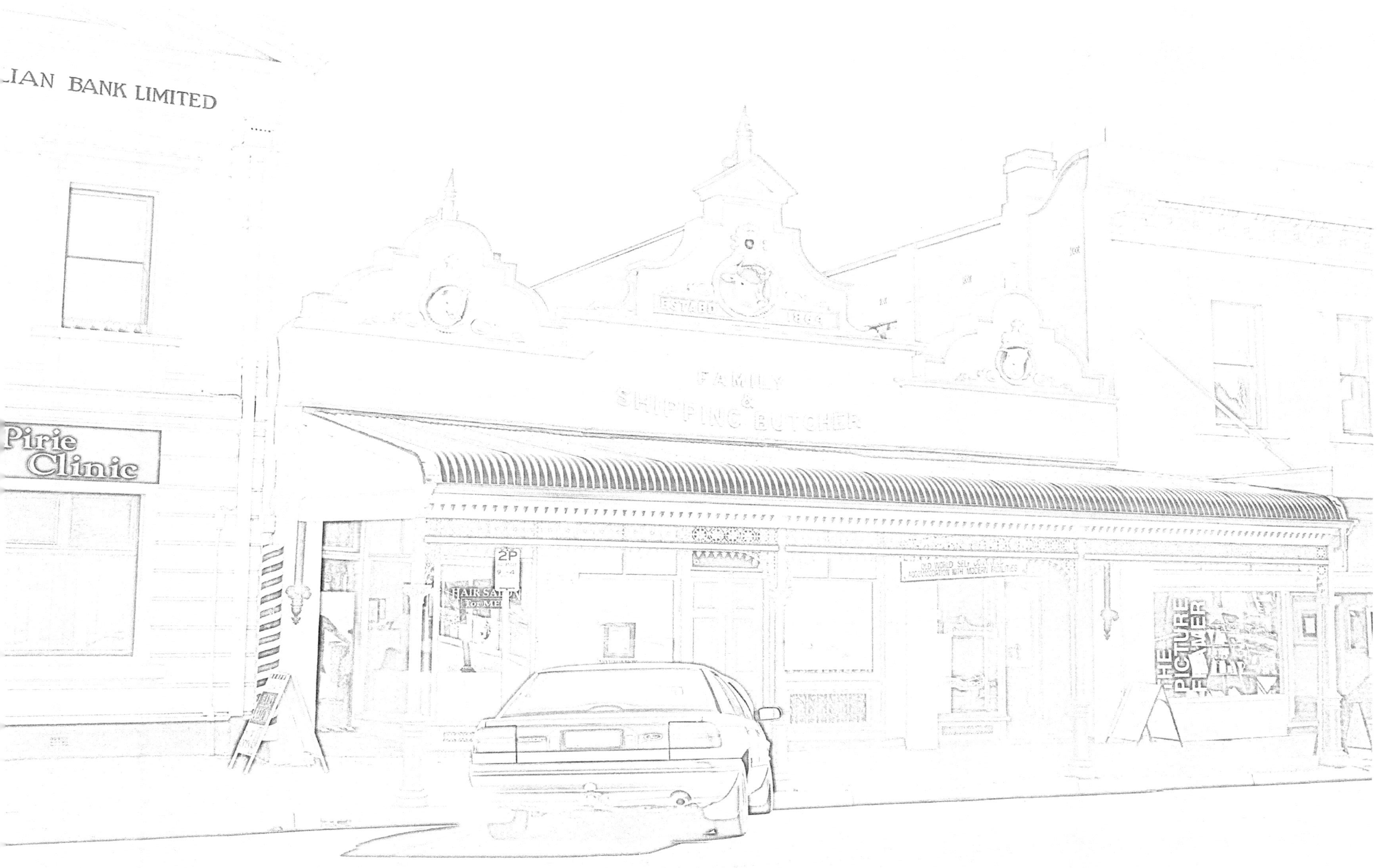
LIAN BANK LIMITED
ESTAB'D
1864
FAMILY
&
SHIPPING BUTCHER
Pirie
Clinic
2P
HAIR SALON
for MEN
THE
PICTURE
FRAMER

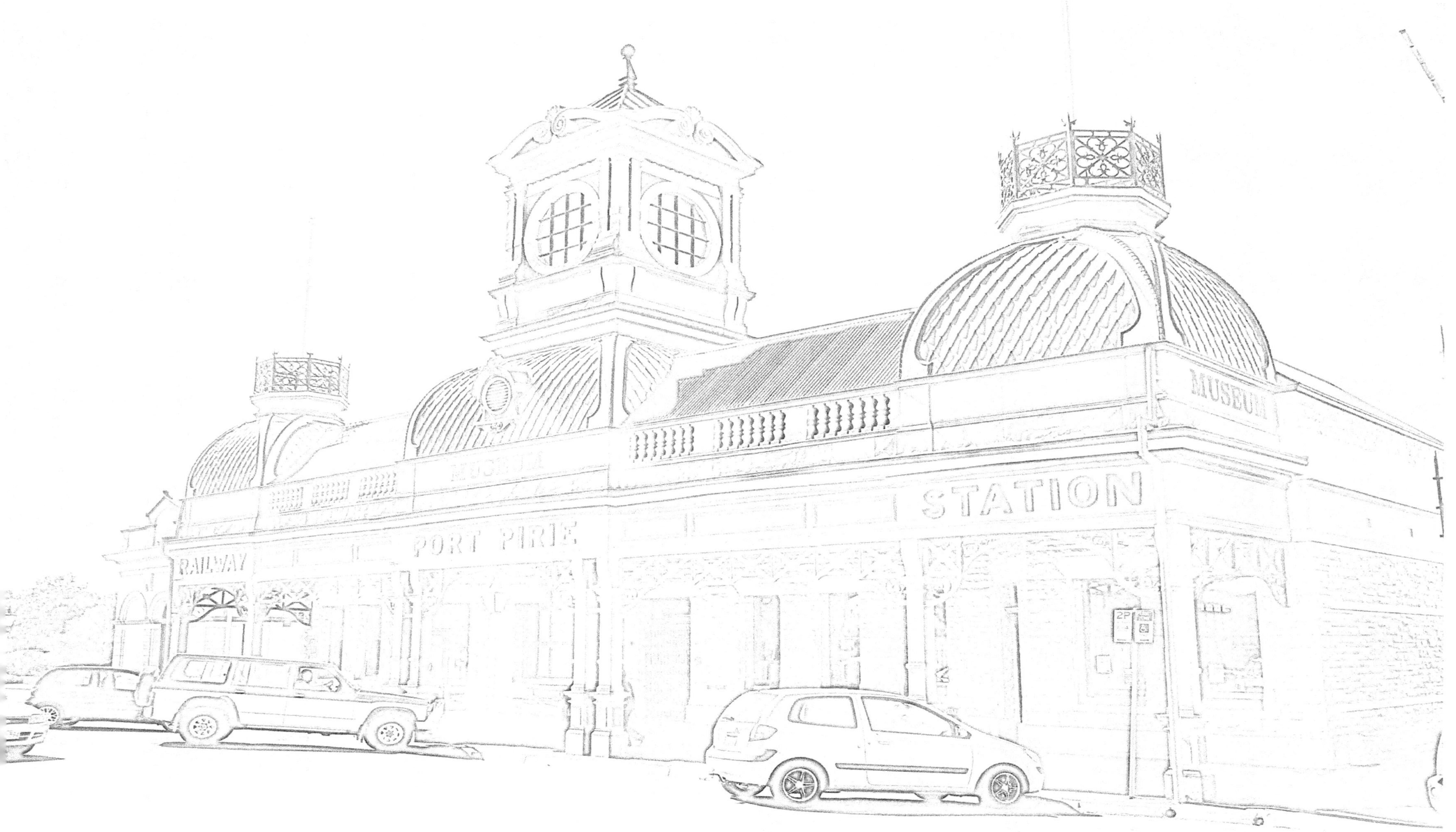
MUSEUM
STATION
PORT PIRIE
RAILWAY
2P

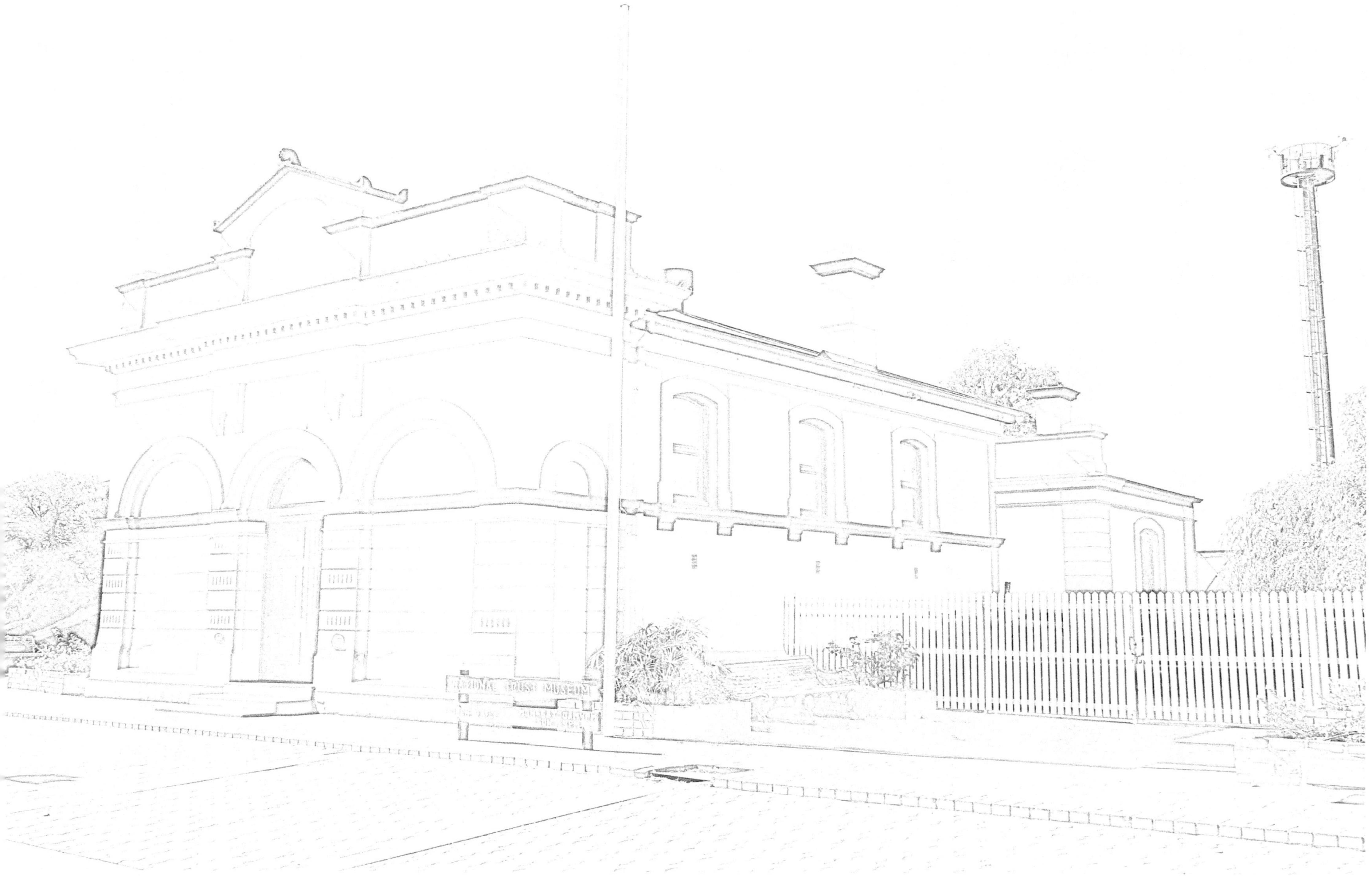
MUSEUM

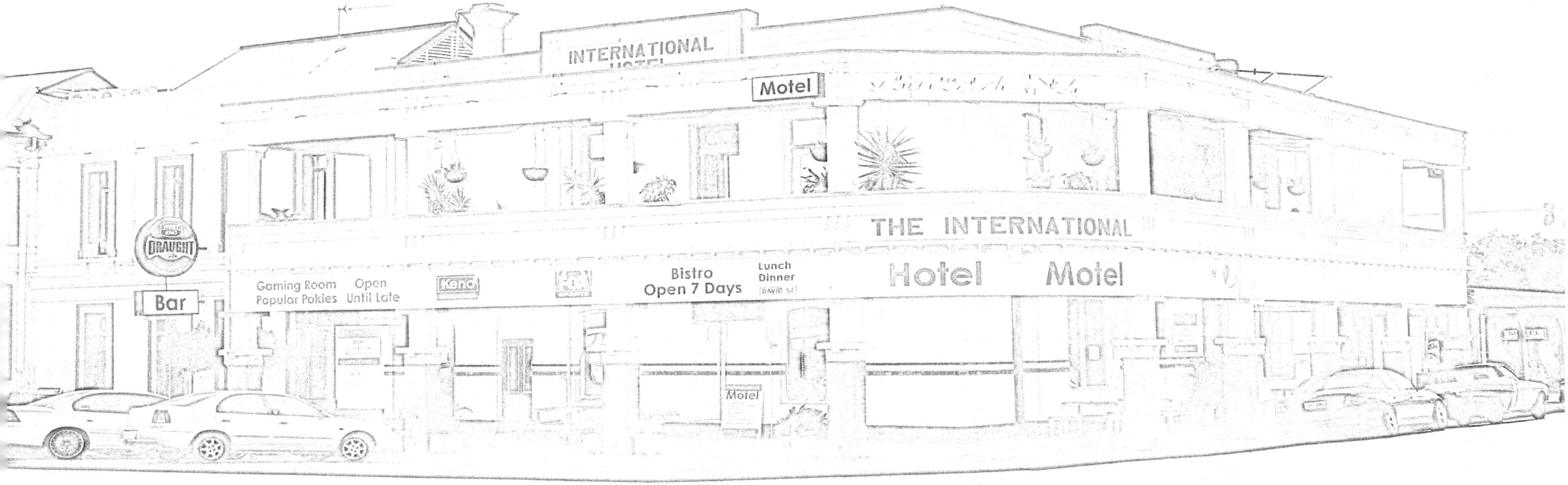
INTERNATIONAL
Motel
THE INTERNATIONAL
DRAUGHT
Bar
Gaming Room
Popular Pokies
Open
Until Late
Keno
Bistro
Open 7 Days
Lunch
Dinner
DAVID ST
Hotel
Motel
Motel

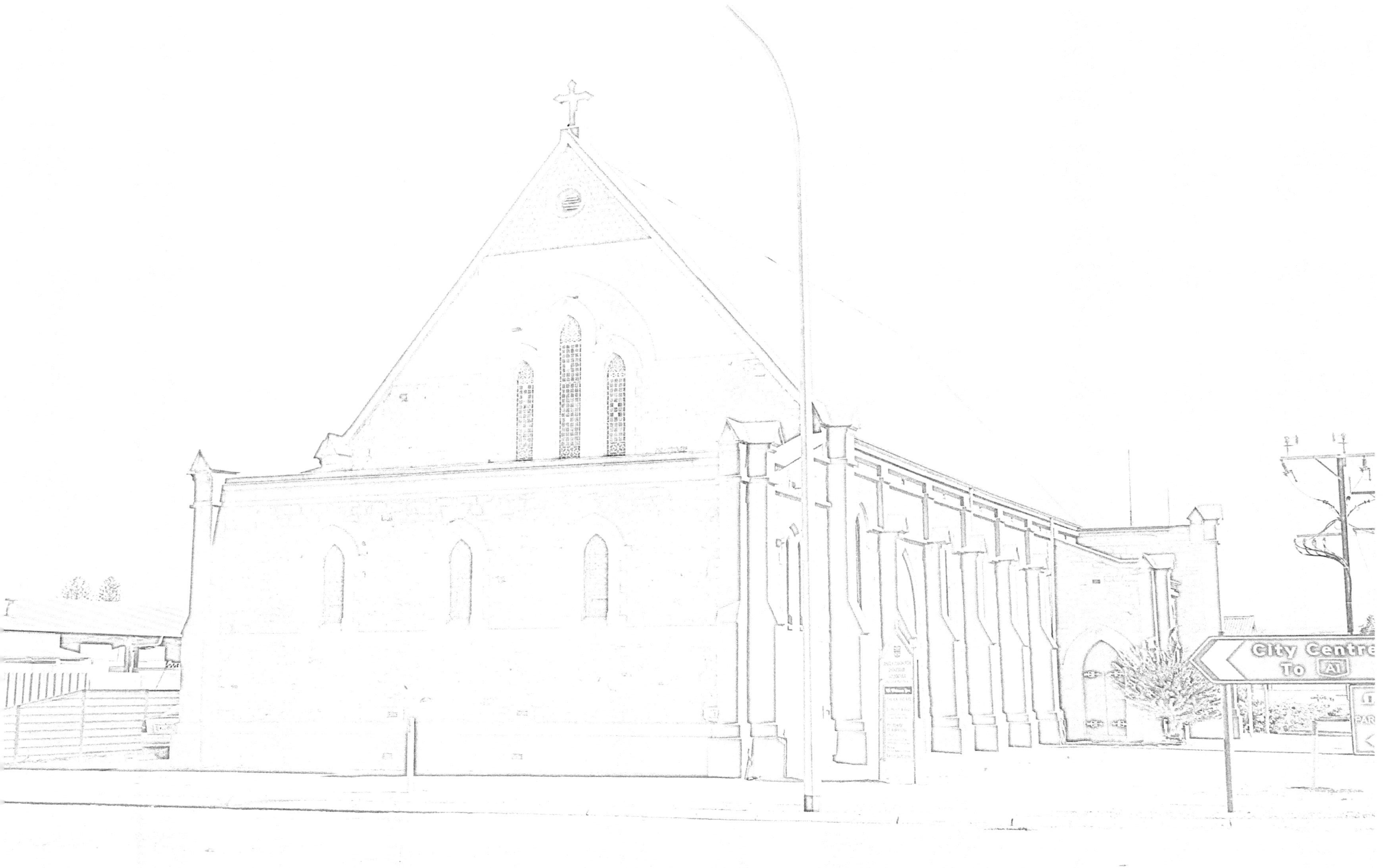

City Centre
To A1

Carn Brae

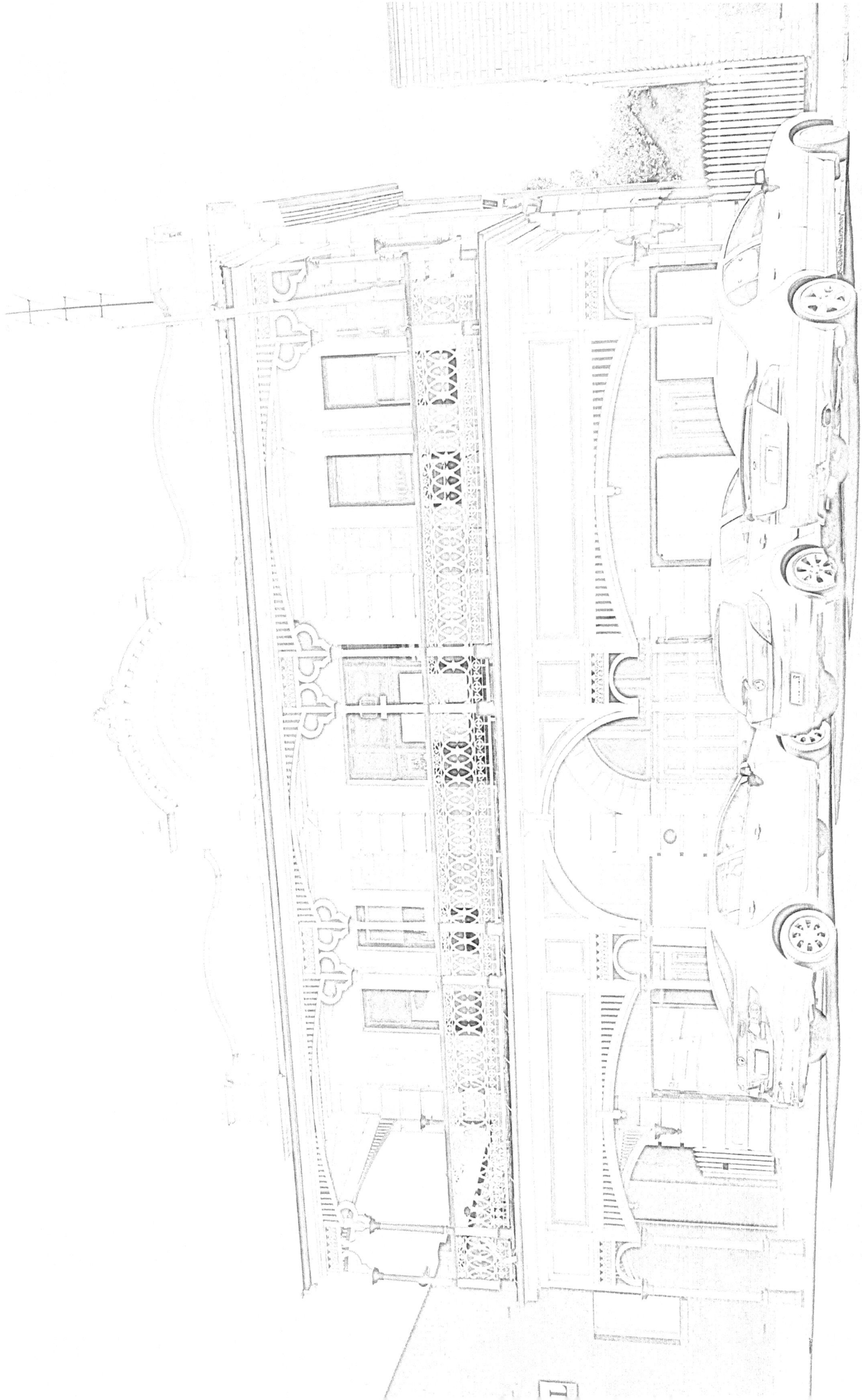

FLINDERS
ARCADE
VKD-667

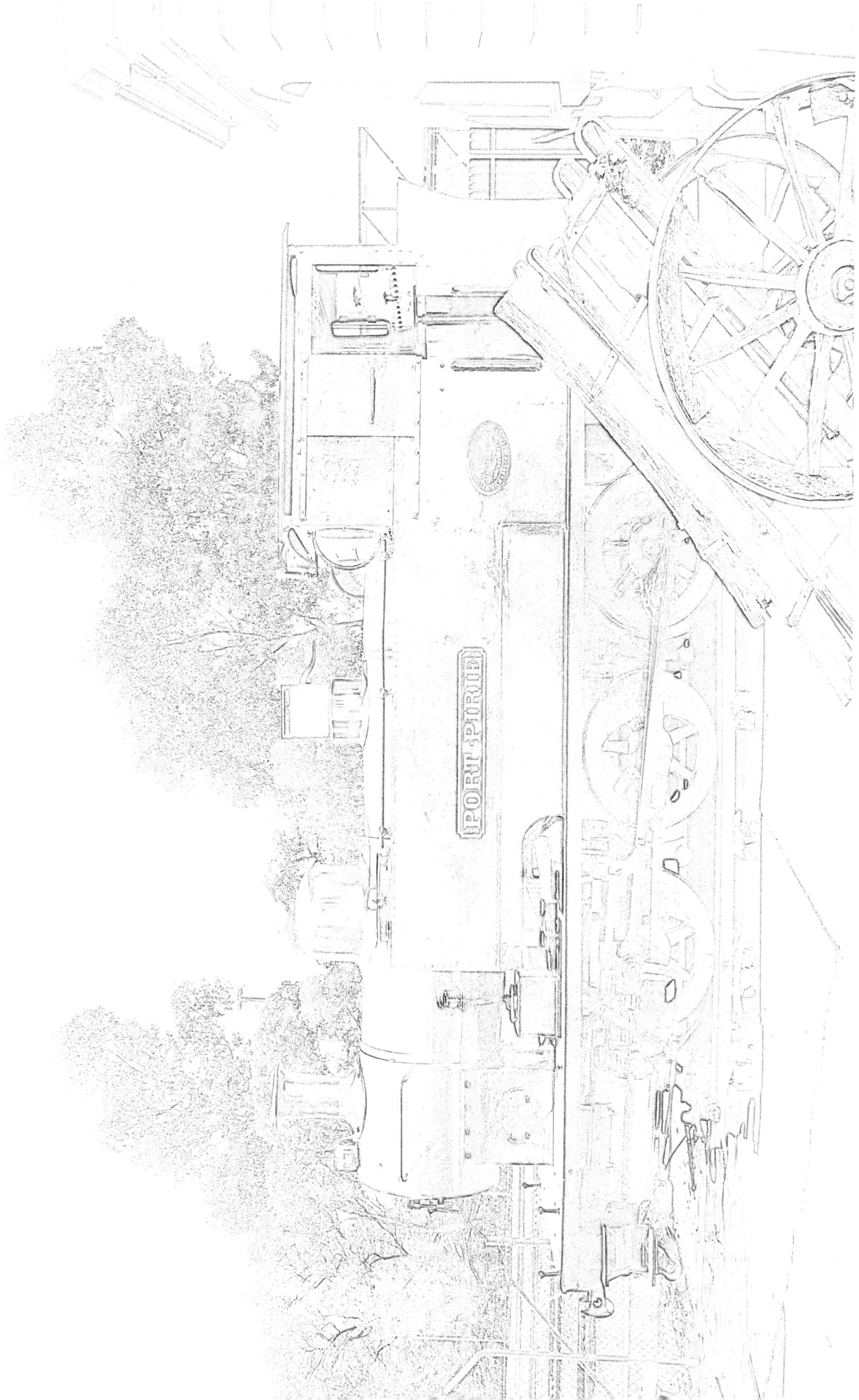
PORT PIRIE

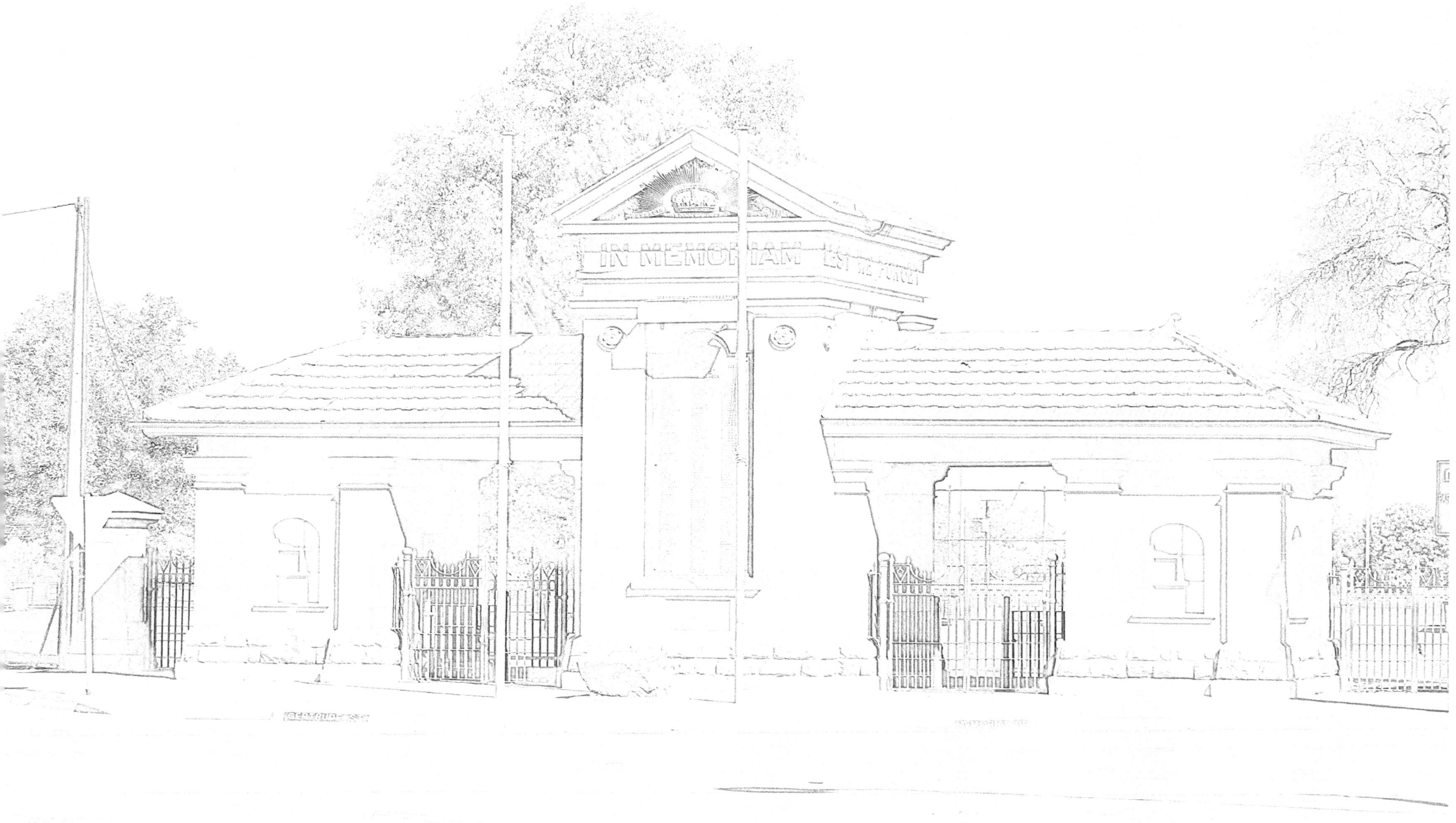
IN MEMORIAM

5

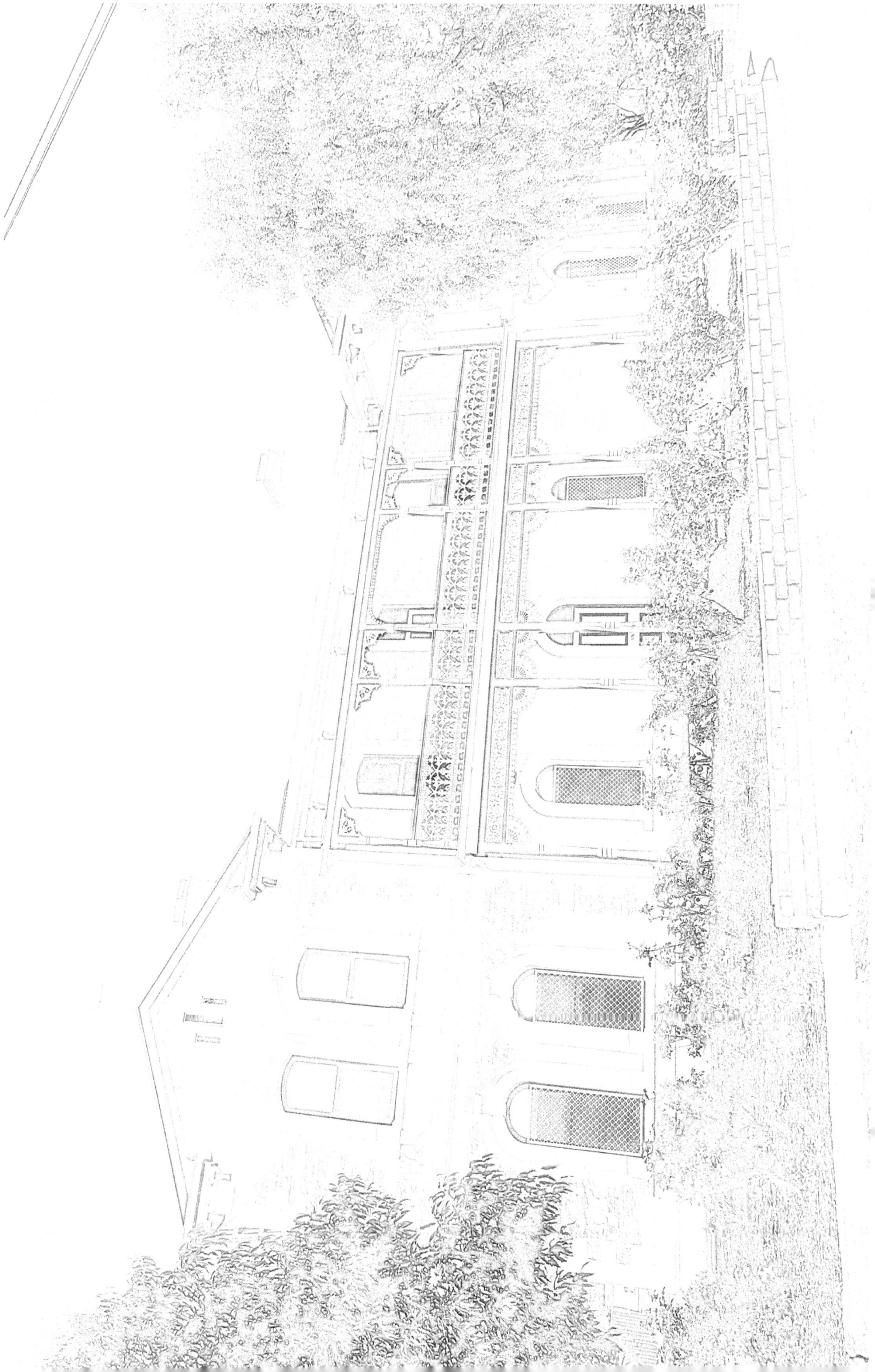

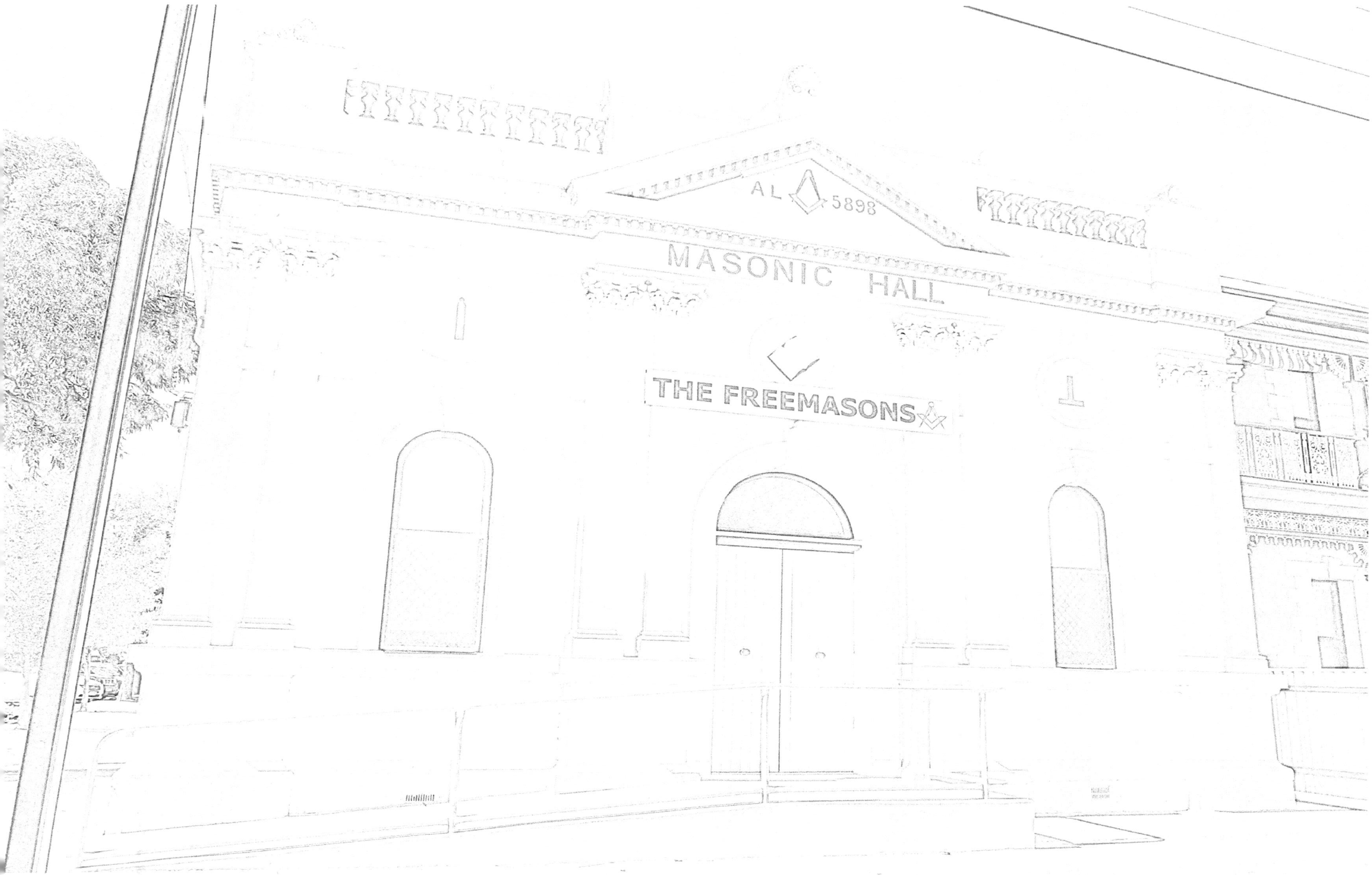
AL 5898
MASONIC HALL
THE FREEMASONS

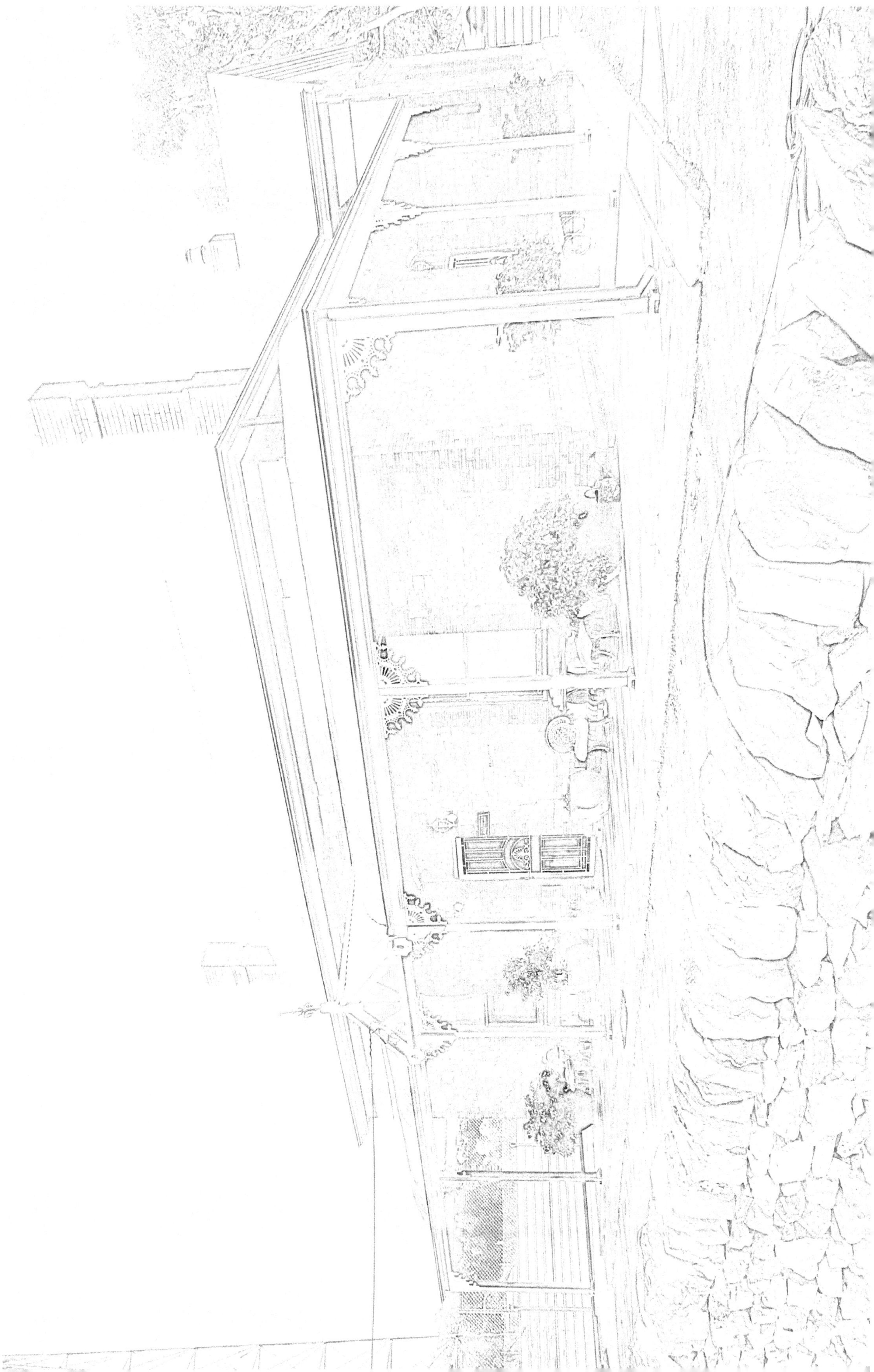

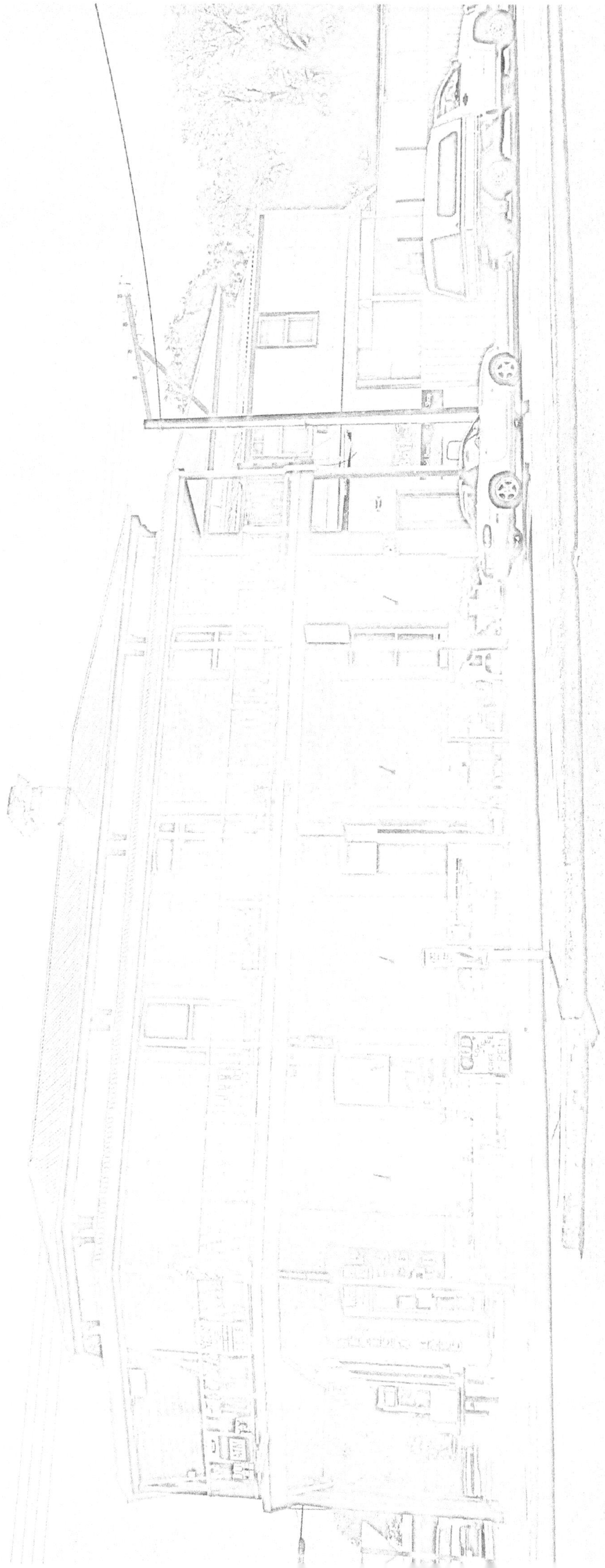

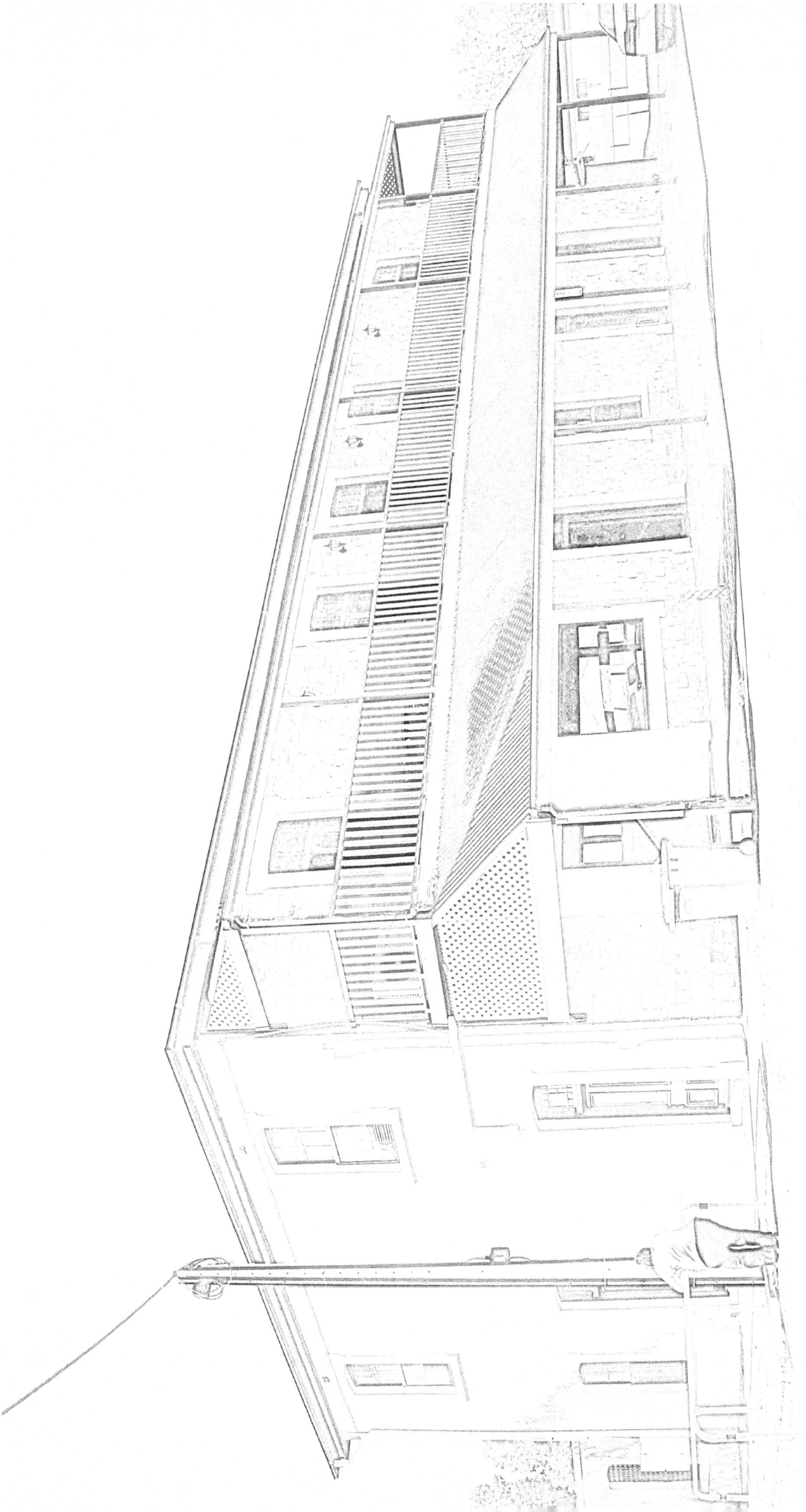

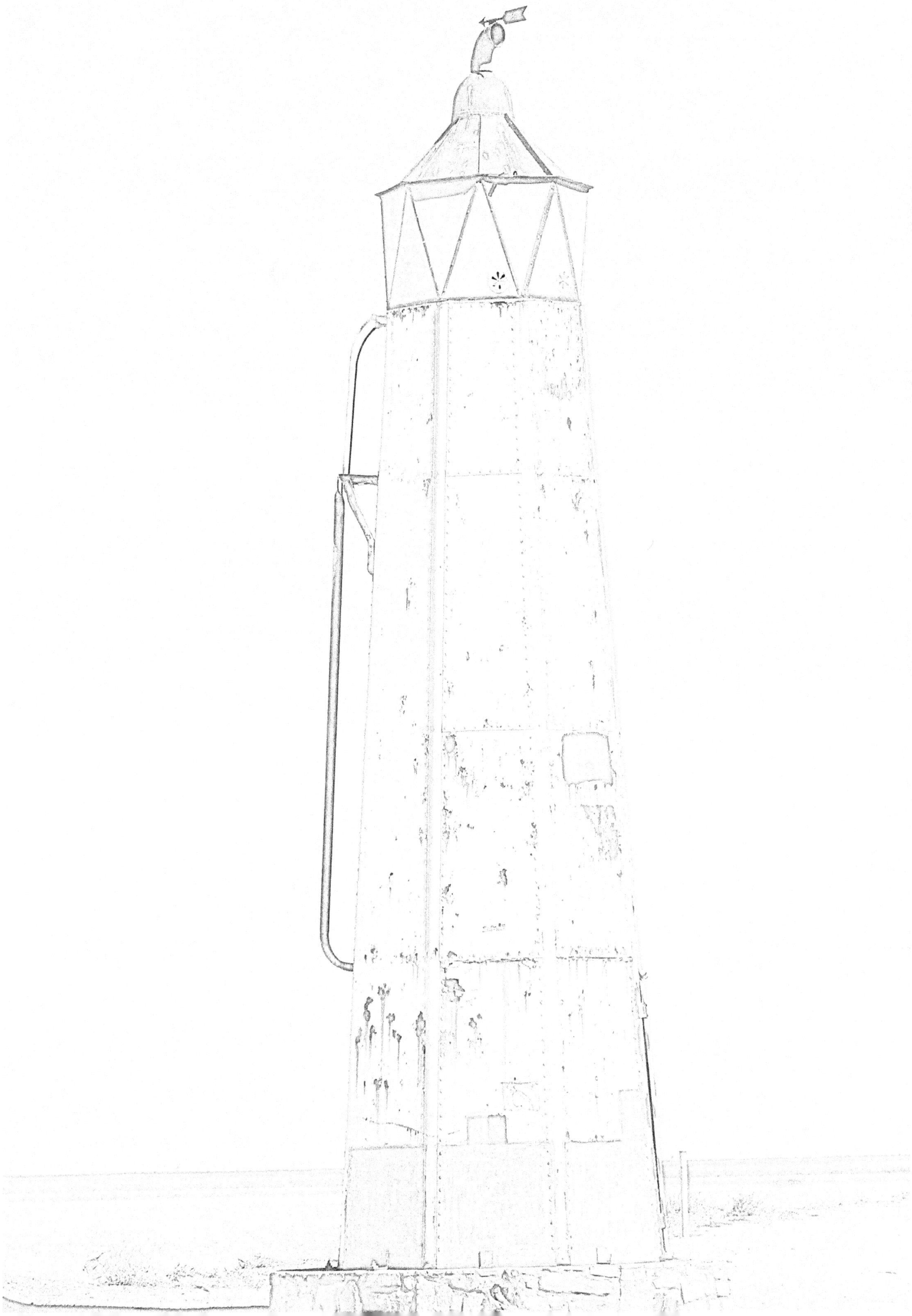

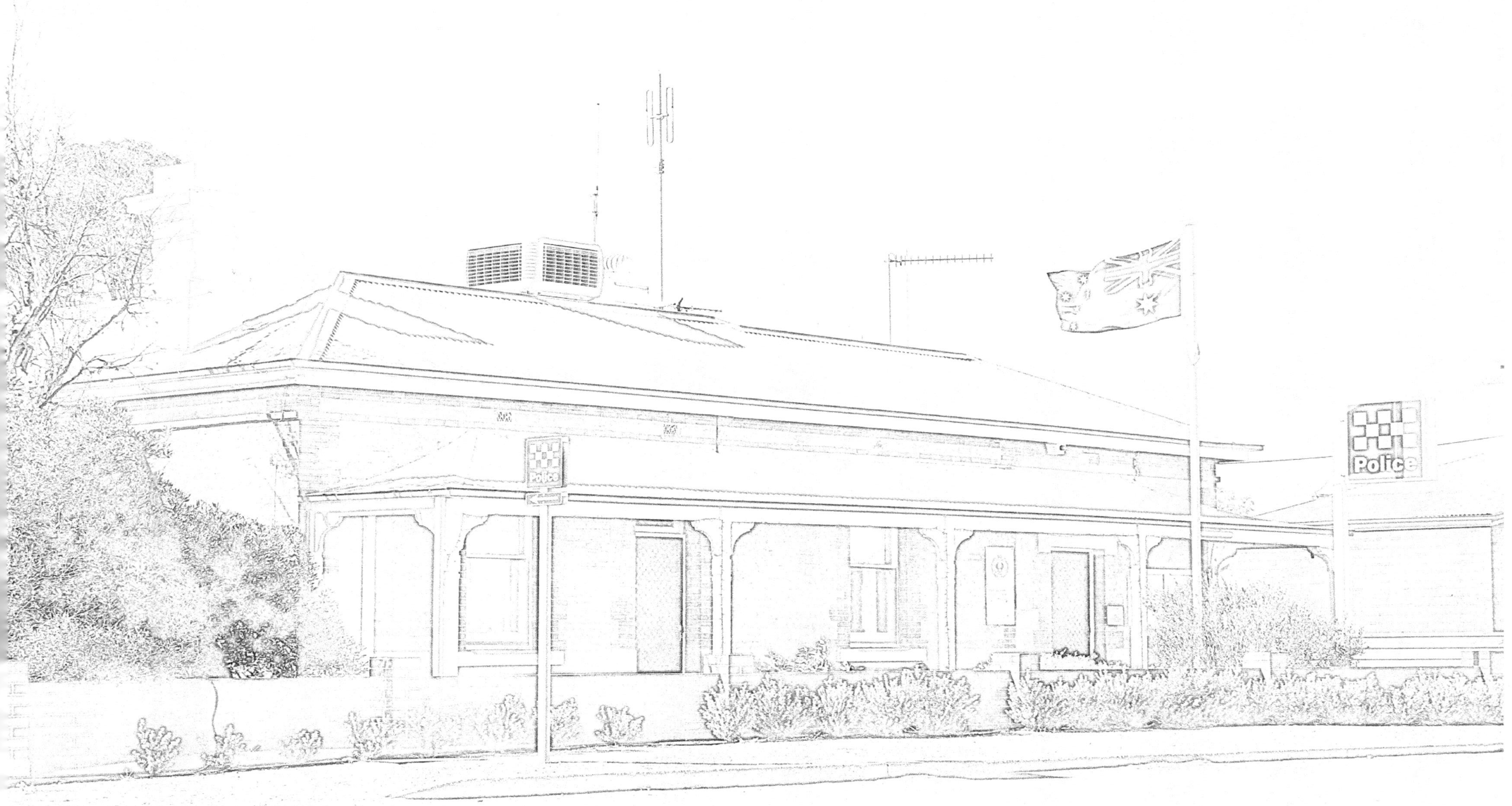
Police
Police

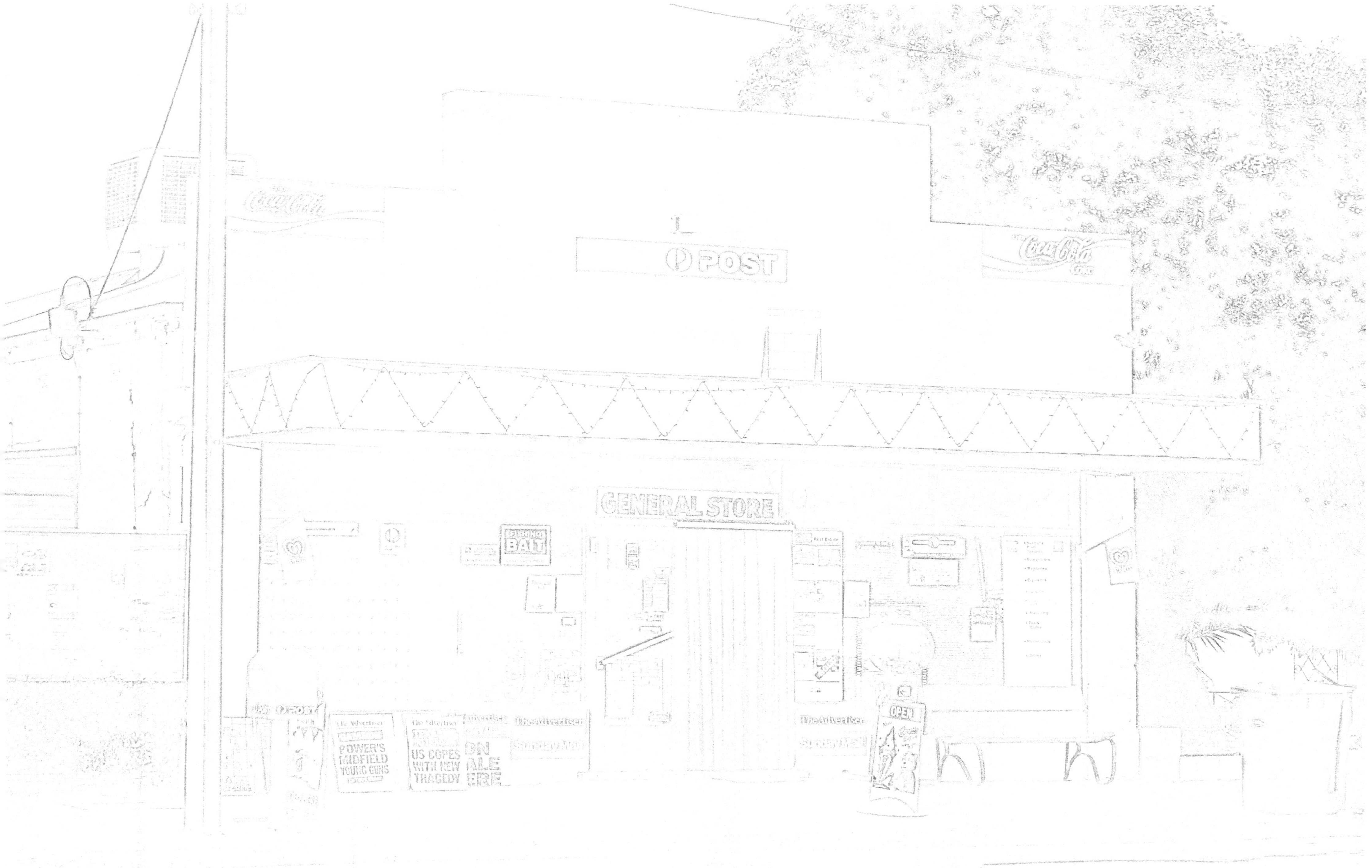

Coca-Cola
POST
Coca-Cola
GENERAL STORE
BAIT
POST
The Advertiser
POWER'S
MIDFIELD
YOUNG GUNS
The Advertiser
US COPES
WITH NEW
TRAGEDY
The Advertiser
Sunday Mail
The Advertiser
Sunday Mail
OPEN

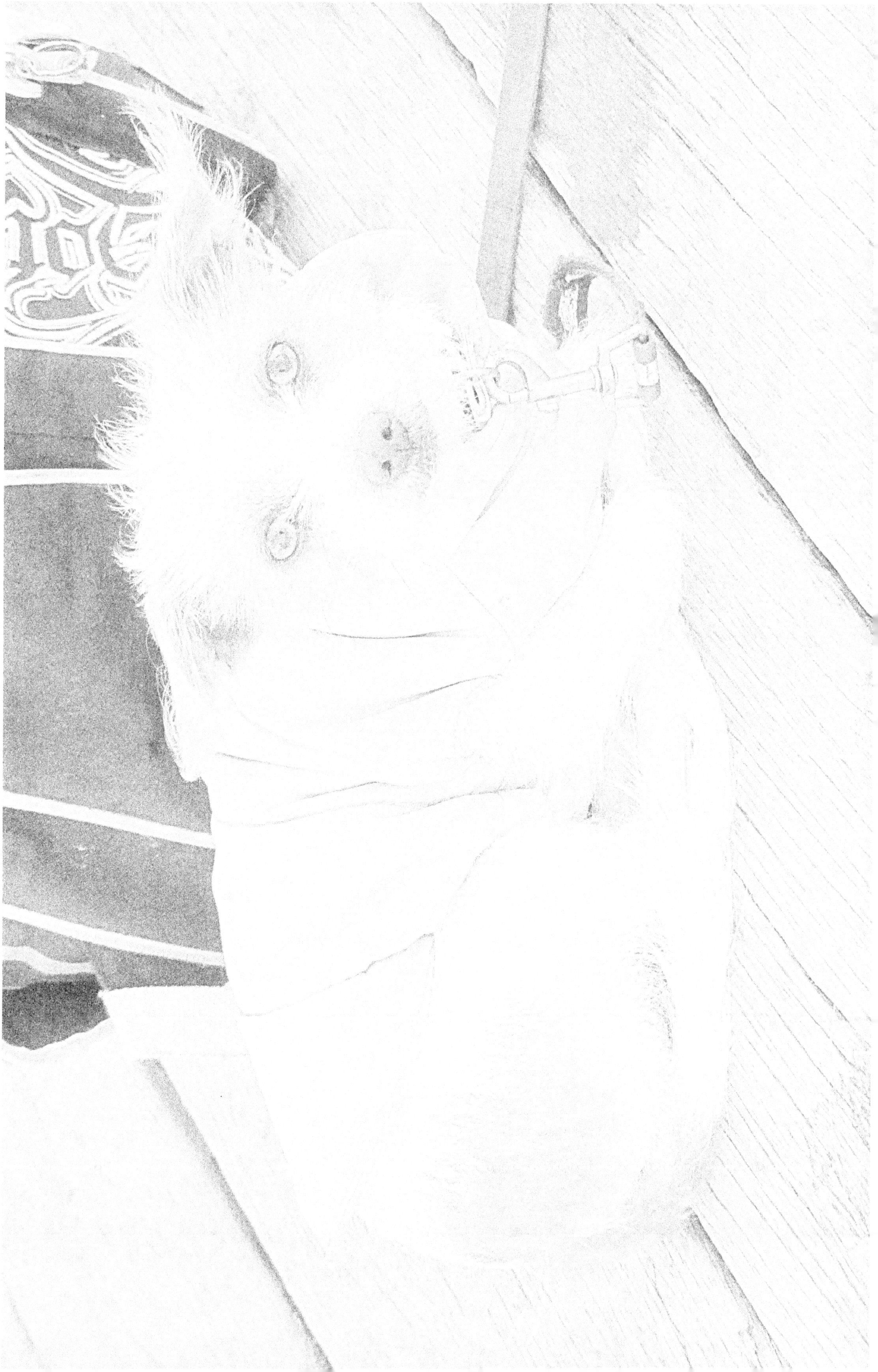

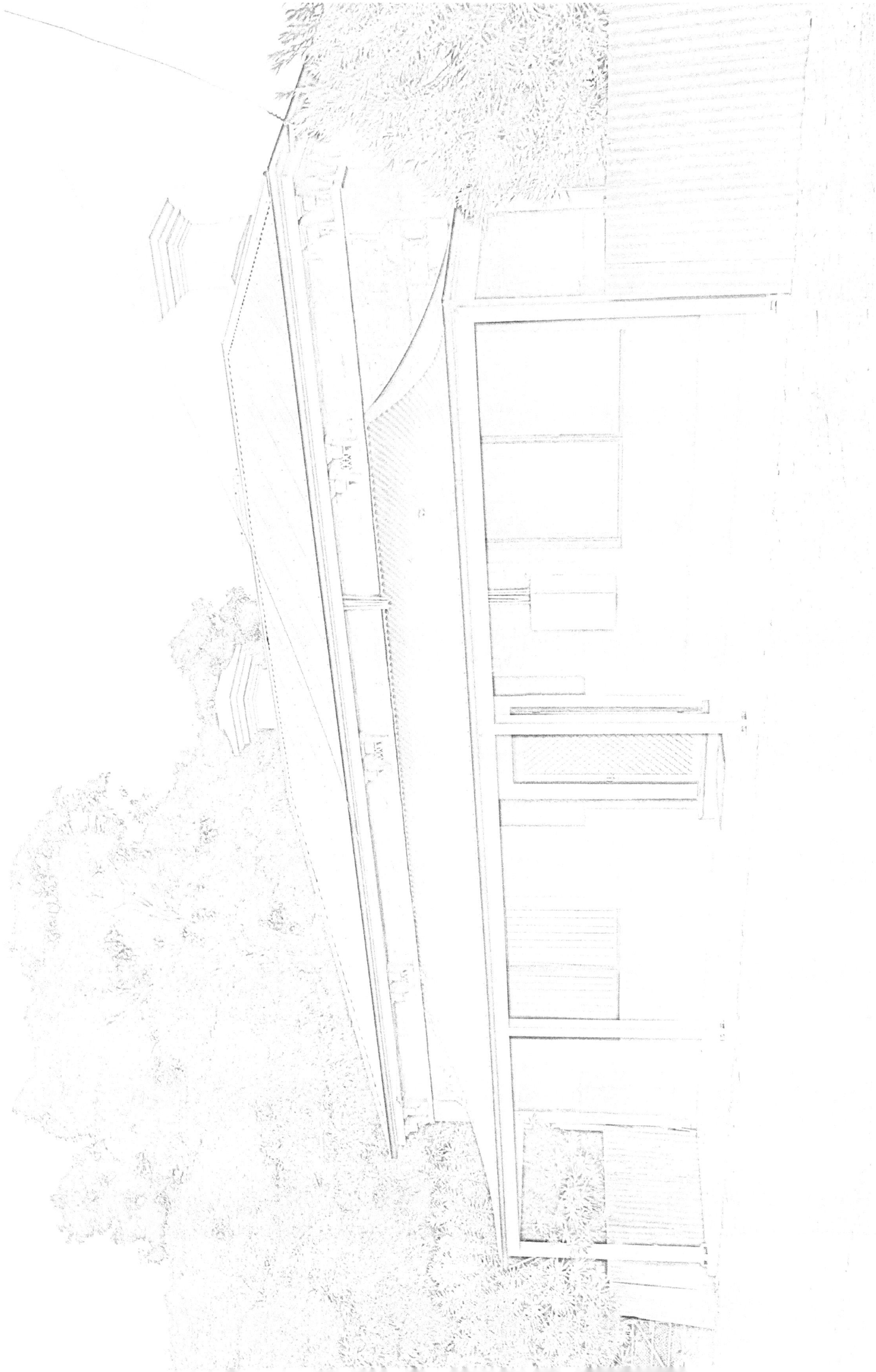

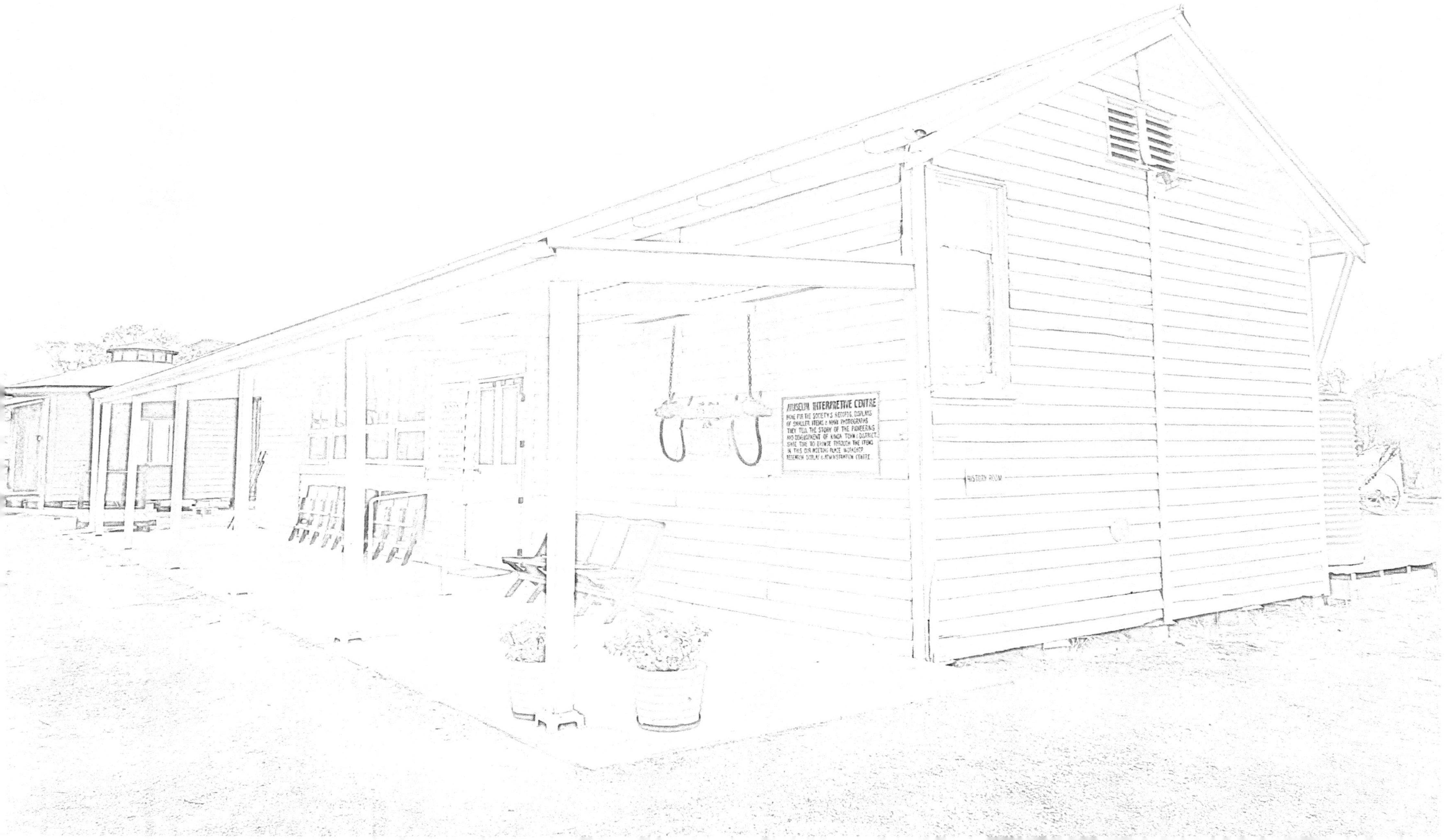
MUSEUM INTERPRETIVE CENTRE

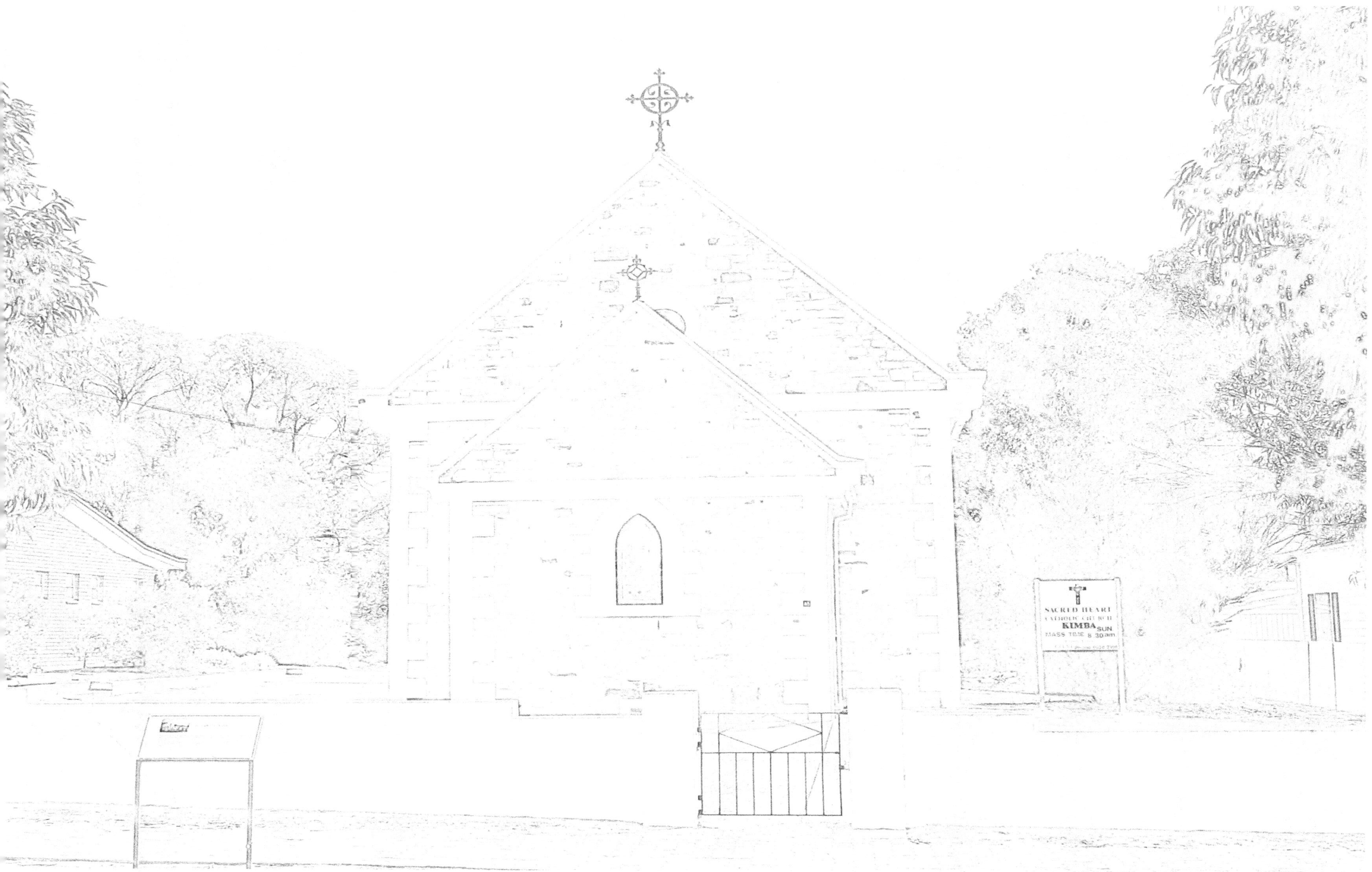
SACRED HEART
KIMBA SUN
MASS
8 30am

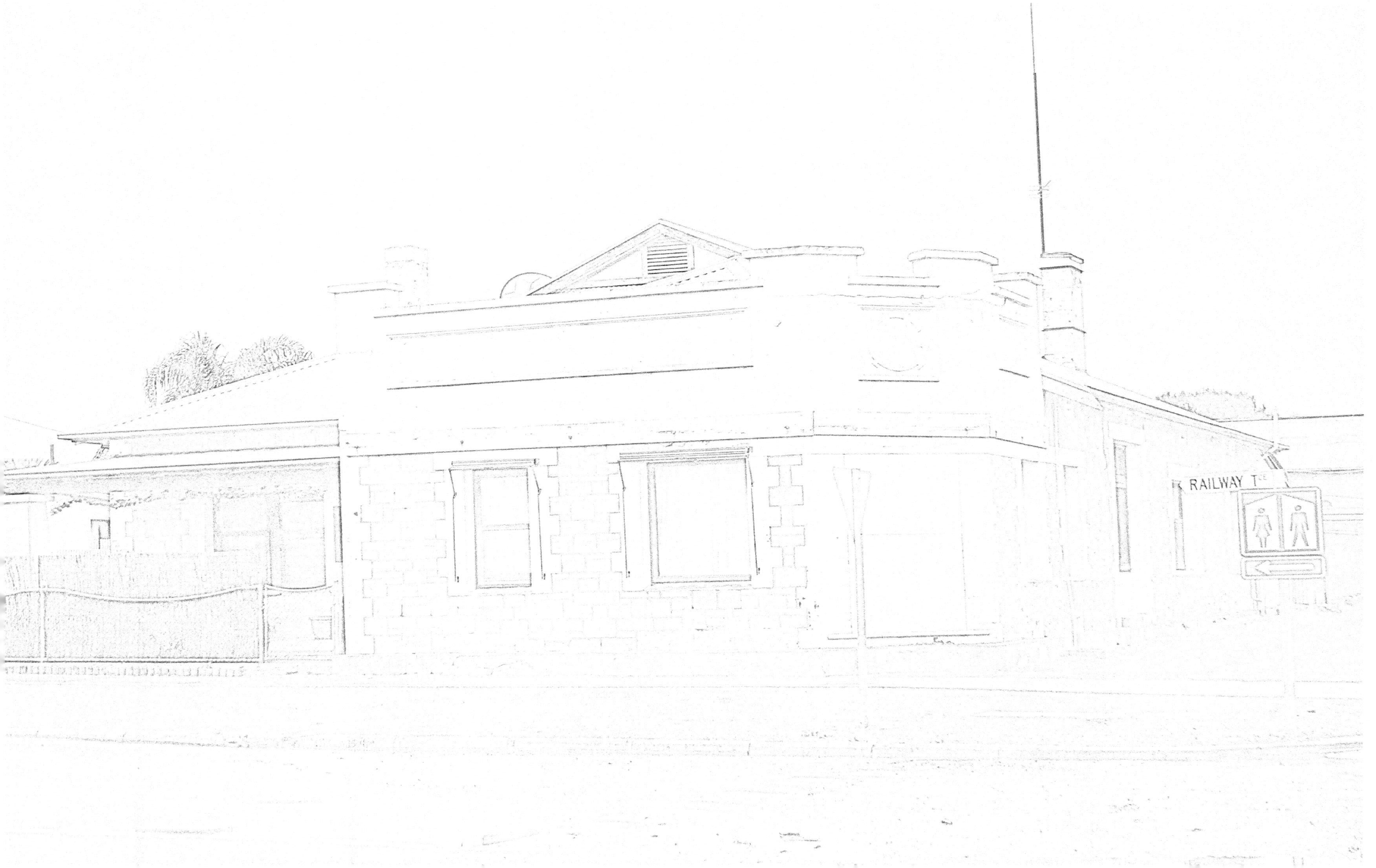
RAILWAY T^CE

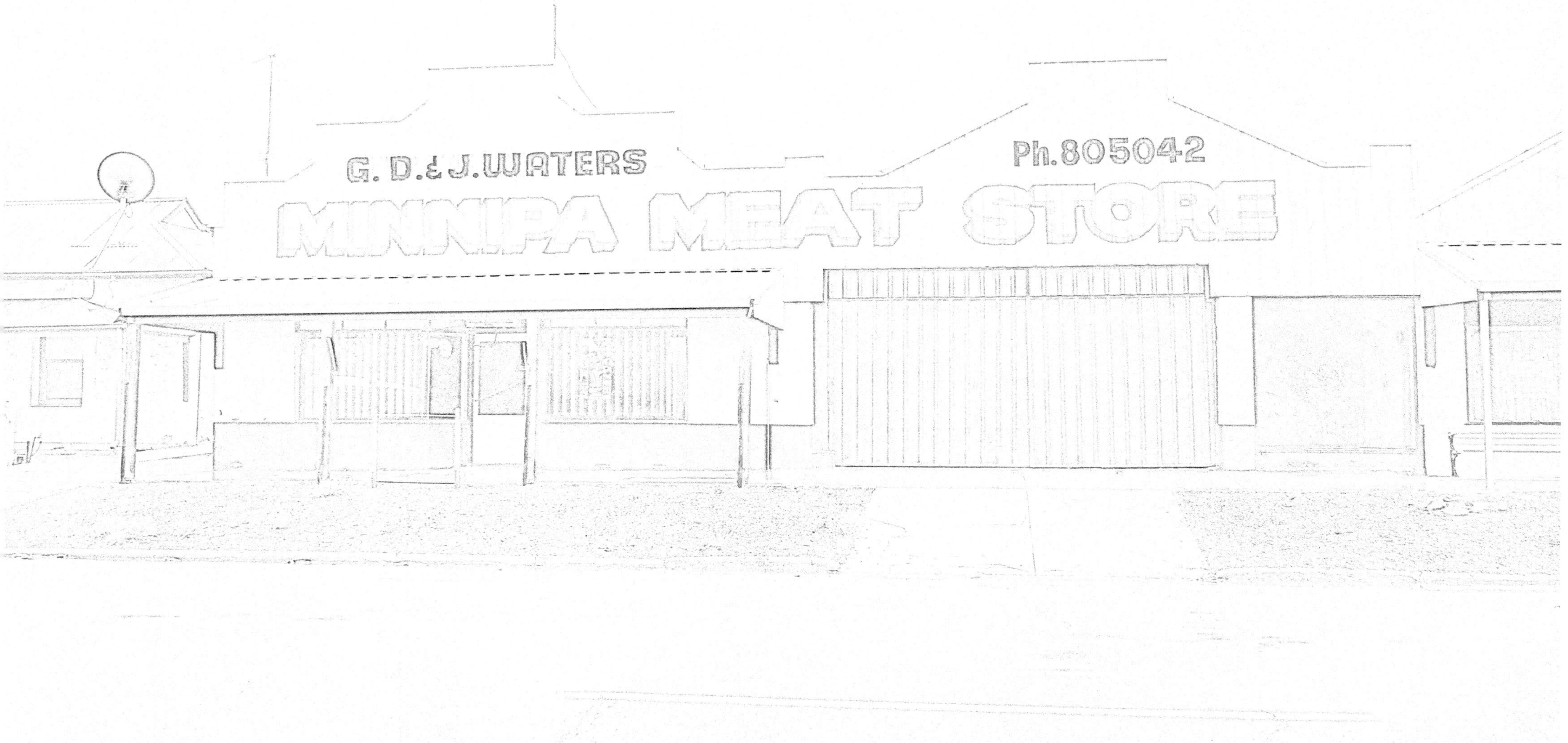
G. D. & J. WATERS
Ph. 805042
MINNIPA MEAT STORE

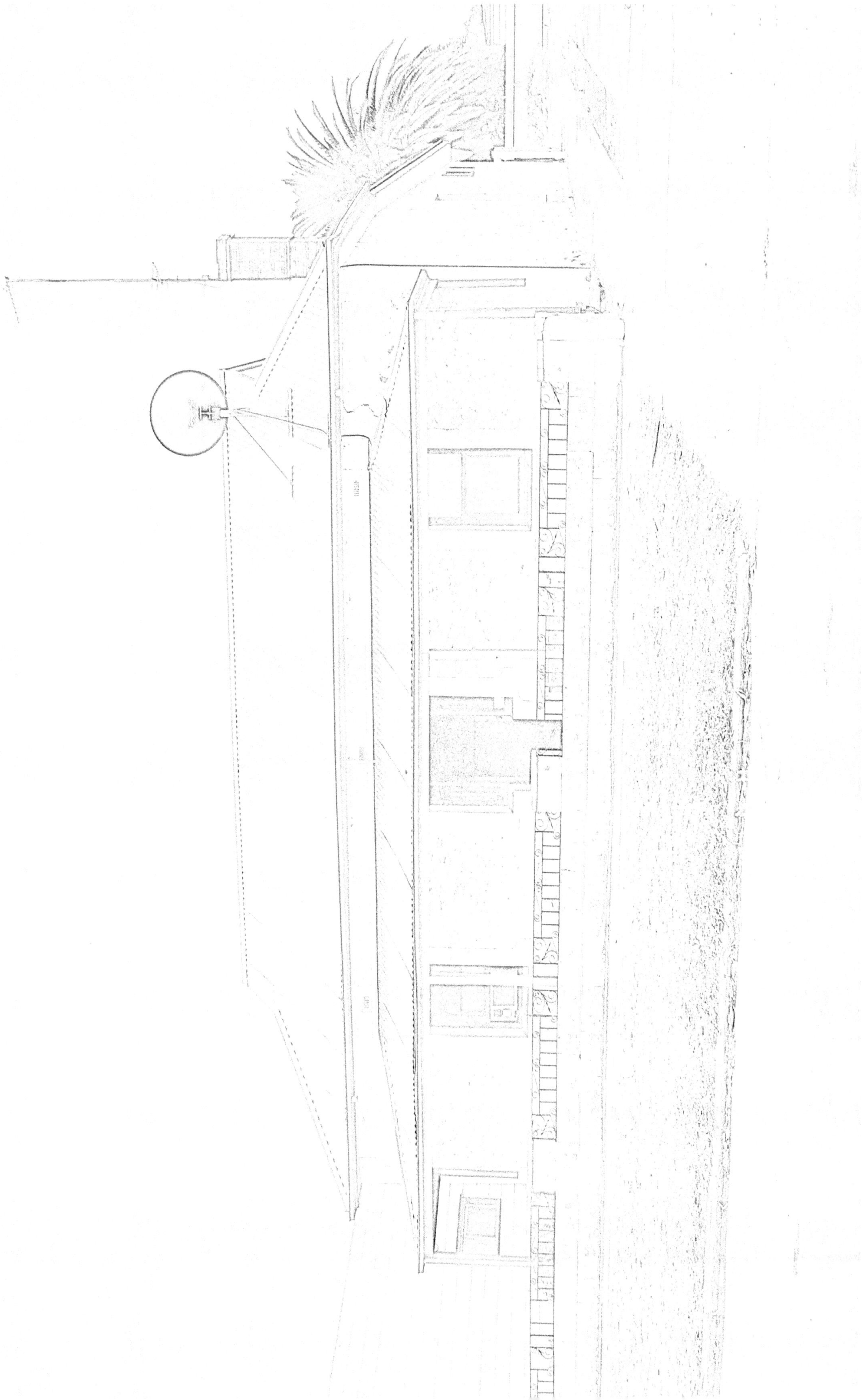

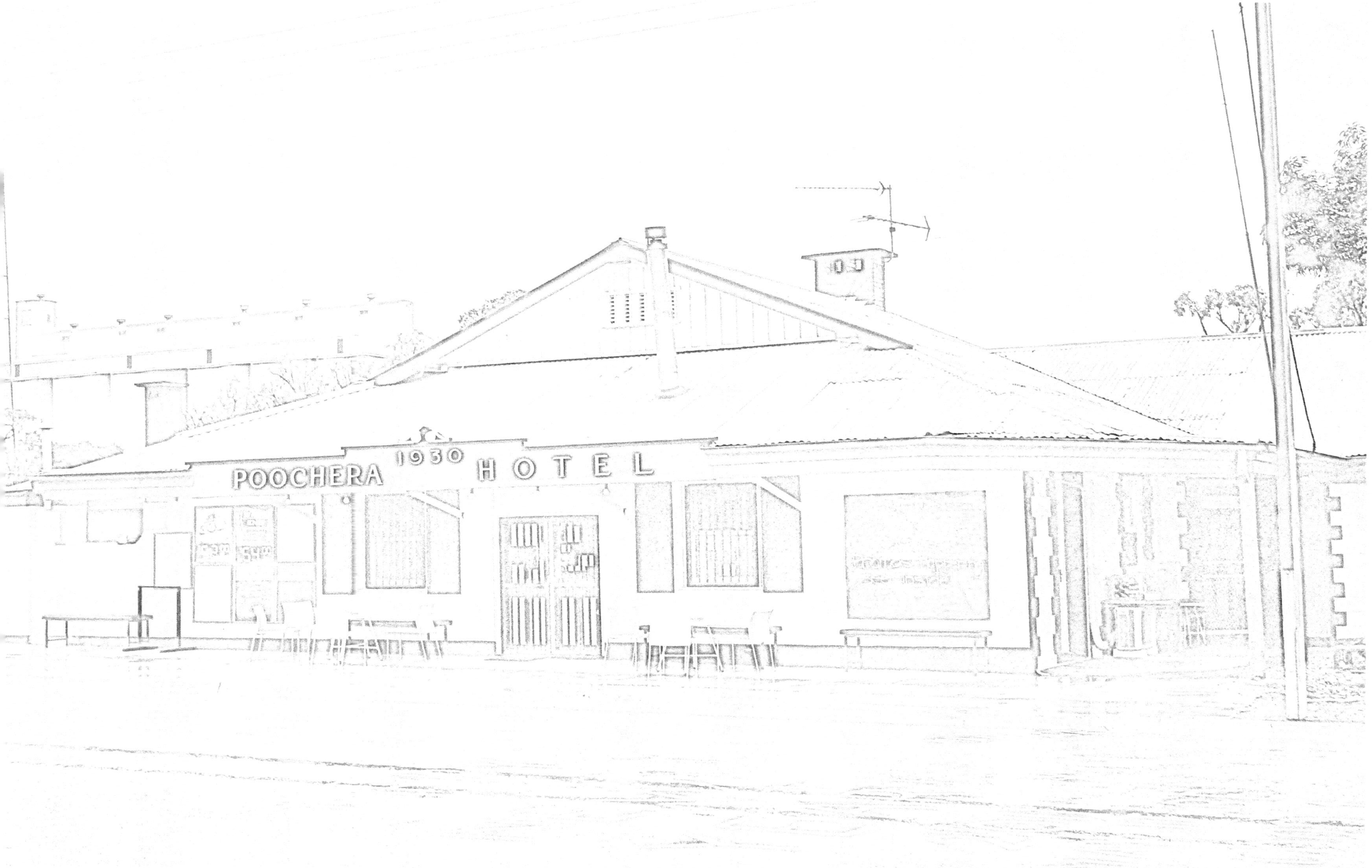
POOCHERA
1930
HOTEL

www.ingramcontent.com/pod-product-compliance
Lightning Source LLC
Chambersburg PA
CBHW081100180526
45170CB00005B/1823
* 9 7 8 0 3 5 9 9 7 2 1 5 9 *